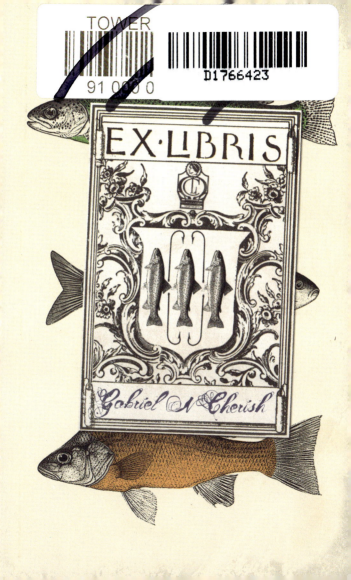

EX·LIBRIS

Gabriel N Cherish

Fishing
A Very
Peculiar
History

With extra maggots

'I sat upon the shore fishing, with the arid
plains behind me.'

The Wasteland, T. S. Eliot

For Chick, Ray, Sean and the chaps
at Whitmore's Lake for help and
encouragement
'RB'

Editor: Jamie Pitman

Published in Great Britain in MMXII by
Book House, an imprint of
The Salariya Book Company Ltd
25 Marlborough Place, Brighton BN1 1UB
www.salariya.com
www.book-house.co.uk

HB ISBN-13: 978-1-908177-91-9

> **WARNING:** The Salariya Book Company accepts
> no responsibility for the recipes in this book. They
> are included only for their historical interest and
> may not be suitable for modern use.

1 3 5 7 9 8 6 4 2
A CIP catalogue record for this book is available
from the British Library.
Printed and bound in Dubai.
Printed on paper from sustainable sources.

Visit our **new** online shop at
shop.salariya.com
for great offers, gift ideas, all our new releases
and free postage and packaging.

Fishing
A Very Peculiar History™

With extra maggots

Written by
Rob Beattie

Created and designed by
David Salariya

'I had been fishing for twenty three years
before I made my first cast for a barbel.
It was a revelation.'
The River Prince, Chris Yates

'In any case, of one thing I am sure –
there is no better psychologist than a
fishing rod on this Earth.'
Fishing Days, Geoffrey Bucknall

'Most anglers regard the catching of
"specimen" fish – big fish – as something
which hardly ever happens.'
Stillwater Angling, Richard Walker

'I realised what I had to do.
Beginning on Anzer, I would fly-fish
from one end of Russia to the other.'
Hooked, Fen Montaigne

'I say dad. It can pull! It's run ten
yards and not stopped yet!'
Fishing with Mr Crabtree in all waters,
Bernard Venables

Contents

British record list

All weights measured using the traditional imperial scale of pounds, ounces and drams.

Barbel 21 pounds, 1 ounce, 0 drams – 2006
Grahame King, Great Ouse, Adams Mill, Beds.

Bleak 0 pounds, 4 ounces, 9 drams – 1998
Dennis Flack, River Lark, Cambridgeshire

Bream (bronze) 19 pounds, 10 ounces, 0 drams – 2005
James Rust, Cambridge stillwater

Bream (silver) 2 pounds, 15 ounces, 0 drams – 2009
Phil Morton, Mill Farm, Pulborough, W. Sussex

Bullhead 0 pounds, 1 ounce, 0 drams – 1983
R. Johnson, Green River, Nr Guildford, Surrey

Carp (mirror/common/leather) 67 pounds, 8 ounces, 0 drams – 2008
Austin Holness, Conningbrook, Nr Ashford, Kent

Carp (crucian) 4 pounds, 9 ounces, 9 drams – 2003
Martin Bowler, Yateley lake, Surrey

Catfish (Wels) 62 pounds, 0 ounces, 0 drams – 1997
Rich Garner, Withy Pool, Henlow, Beds.

Char (Arctic) 9 pounds, 8 ounces, 0 drams – 1995
W. Fairbairn, Loch Arkaig, Inverness, Scotland

Chub 9 pounds, 5 ounces, 0 drams – 2007
Andy Maker, Southern stillwater

Dace 1 pound, 5 ounces, 2 drams – 2002
Simon Ashton, River Wear, Co. Durham

Eel 11 pounds, 2 ounces, 0 drams – 1978
Steve Terry, Kingfisher Lake, Nr Ringwood, Hants.

Grayling 4 pounds, 3 ounces, 0 drams – 1989
S. R. Lanigan, River Frome, Dorset

Gudgeon 0 pounds, 5 ounces, 0 drams – 1990
D. H. Hull, River Nadder, Sutton Mandeville, Wilts.

Perch 6 pounds, 3 ounces, 0 drams – 2011
Neill Stephen, Stream Valley Lakes, E. Sussex

Pike 46 pounds, 13 ounces, 0 drams – 1992
Roy Lewis, Llandegfedd Reservoir, S. Wales

Roach 4 pounds, 4 ounces, 0 drams – 2006
Keith Berry, Northern Ireland stillwater.

Rudd 4 pounds, 10 ounces, 0 drams – 2001
Simon Parry, Freshwater Lake, Co. Armagh, NI
4 pounds, 10 ounces, 0 drams – 2001
Simon Parry, Clay Lake, Co. Armagh, NI

Ruffe 0 pounds, 5 ounces, 4 drams – 1980
R. J. Jenkins, West View Farm, Cumbria

Salmon 64 pounds, 0 ounces, 0 drams – 1922
G. W. Ballatine, River Tay, Scotland

Tench 15 pounds, 3 ounces, 6 drams – 2001
Darren Ward, Sheepwalk big pit, Shepperton, Middlesex

Trout (brown) 31 pounds, 12 ounces, 0 drams – 2002
Brian Rutland, Loch Awe, Argyll, Scotland

Trout (rainbow) 33 pounds, 3 ounces, 0 drams – 2003
J. Lawson, Watercress Trout Fishery, Devon

Trout (sea) 28 pounds, 5 ounces, 4 drams – 1992
J. Farrent, Calshot Spit, River Test, Hampshire

Zander 21 pounds, 5 ounces, 0 drams – 2007
James Benfield, River Severn at Upper Lode

> To read a fishing book is the next best thing to fishing. It is like talk in the fishing inn at night.

Rod and Line, Arthur Ransome

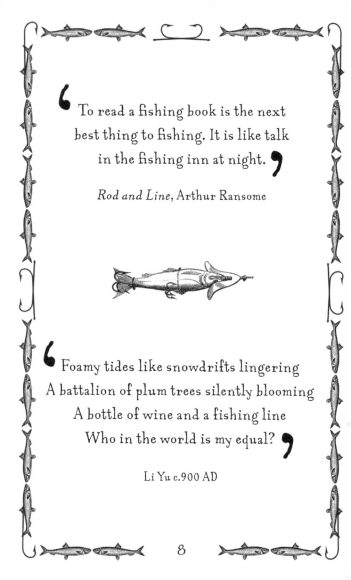

> Foamy tides like snowdrifts lingering
> A battalion of plum trees silently blooming
> A bottle of wine and a fishing line
> Who in the world is my equal?

Li Yu c.900 AD

FIRST CASTS

You don't choose fishing. Fishing chooses you. There comes a moment in every angler's life when the things around them – the water, the wind at their back, the sun on their shoulders, the float that was dancing merrily down the steam and is now suddenly gone – fall into place, like the pieces of a puzzle. At that moment, everything makes sense – even the things that don't make sense. And whether you catch that fish or the next one or the one after that, you know it will never be enough. An angler you shall be.

9

Early evidence

Mankind has been catching and eating fish since records began – though it was considered a food of pretty much last resort by Homer in the *Odyssey*.[1] Fishing has also been used instructively – witness Job's admonishment that he may as well 'try and catch Leviathan with a hook as thwart God's will', a reference that also persuades scholars it wasn't just nets that were being cast out to sea.

As well as wriggling on the end of a line or served up steaming on a plate with a few fresh greens, fish have traditionally enjoyed a rich symbolic life. We're told that they were the first creatures to appear when the earth was created, Jesus chose them to demonstrate a miracle at the feeding of the 5,000, and later, *ichthys*, the Greek word for fish, was adapted as a cipher for '*Iesous Christos Theou Yios Soter*' or 'Jesus Christ, God's Son, Saviour' and used as a sort of secret handshake when persecuted Christians met for the first time.

---

1. Only when 'famine was oppressing their belly' do the heroes of the Odyssey resort to eating fish. And no one in the Iliad goes near them.

Perhaps when early man caught and ate fish, he was after more than simply sustenance? Fish turn up all over Europe as symbols for wisdom and it's clear that the Celts felt that the salmon in particular might even have powers of prophecy. Maybe that's why the salmon occupies such an elevated position among modern anglers; it certainly helps to explain why salmon anglers think they're better than the rest of us.

Species profile: The bleak

Irritating little silver fish found in rivers that grows to a few ounces and specialises in taking baits meant for its more interesting (and usually larger) brothers and sisters. Inexperienced eyes may mistake it for a small dace but while that has an attractive, subtle colouring and an air of purpose, the bleak resembles a tiny herring that hasn't a clue what it's doing.

Good for: Nothing (oh alright, it's good for beginners).

Here comes the hook

Early hooks were actually small pieces of bone, horn, shell or stone sharpened at both ends, smeared with something tasty and then tied to the end of a cord or sinew which was in turn either held in the hand or secured to the bank. Toss it in the water and when the fish tries to swallow it, the line pulls taut and the business end (or gorge) gets caught in the fish's throat. Interestingly, the device used by modern anglers to remove hooks is still called a disgorger.

Easter Island

One of the lesser mysteries of Easter Island or Rapa Nui (i.e. not the one about the enormous stone heads) is how there came to be so many complete bone hooks and hook fragments discovered there – since there are no large mammals indigenous to the island. Some believe the rich source of bone can be traced back to our old friend, human sacrifice, which was commonly practised until missionaries arrived at the turn of the last century and put a stop to it; others credit a clever young fisherman called Urevaiaus, who raided his father's tomb and made hooks out of his thigh bone.

It's also been suggested that thorns may have been used as early hooks, while we know that Native Americans made use of the claws and beaks of birds of prey to catch fish in the same way. The Scandinavians were also fond of a good hook, as archaeological finds near Stavanger, Norway testify; these bone hooks are between seven thousand and eight thousand years old and rudimentary compared with later discoveries from down the road near Bergen, which demonstrate beautiful workmanship and are some of the earliest hooks to feature barbs.

By 2,000 BC, the Egyptians were – as usual – miles ahead of the rest of the ancient world. Tombs from the 12th dynasty depict men fishing with rod, line and hook (probably made of copper, without a barb) a good thousand years before even the Chinese got in on the act. By the Middle Ages, hook-making had become a saleable skill and far-sighted anglers had also begun to realise that you didn't have to bait a hook to catch a fish – you could also disguise it as something they liked to eat. Fly fishing was born.

13

Aelfric's Colloquy

– being the attempt of a Dorset monk living at the end of the 10th century to encourage his pupils to learn Latin. He came up with the racy idea of a series of dialogues, written in Anglo-Saxon, with a Latin translation.

Teacher: What skills do you have?
Fisherman: I am a fisherman.
Teacher: What do you gain from your skills?
Fisherman: I get food, clothes and money.
Teacher: How do you catch the fish?
Fisherman: I get into my boat, put my nets into the river and then I cast my bait and wicker baskets, and whatever I catch I take.
Teacher: What if the fish are unclean ones?[1]
Fisherman: I throw out the unclean ones and I take the clean ones for food for myself.
Teacher: Where do you sell your fish?
Fisherman: In the town.
Teacher: Who buys them?
Fisherman: The townsfolk. I cannot catch as many as I can sell.
Teacher: What sort of fish do you catch?
Fisherman: I catch eels, pike, minnows and dace, trout, lamprey and any other species that swim in the river, like sprats.

---

1. *According to Leviticus, chapter 11, verse 12: 'Whatever in the water does not have fins or scales; that shall be an abomination to you.' Mr Lamprey, j'accuse.*

14

fishing in the 15th century

If you were interested in angling in the late 1400s, there was only one game in town – a remarkable how-to book called *A treatyse of fysshynge wyth an Angle*, said to have been written by the prioress of a nunnery in St Albans, just north of London. Dam Julyans Barnes may have had strong religious convictions, but these didn't preclude her from continuing to enjoy more earthly pursuits like hunting, hawking and fishing. The piscatorial prioress explains how to make a rod (the wood must be a fathom and a half long (2.74 metres) and cut between Michelmas and Candlemas[1]), how to choose your line (the longest and fairest hair from a horse tail is best), colour it (ale and soot make a good brown line), and then goes on to tell you which colour line to use at which time of the year. She talks about hooks, how to match them to the right line and size them depending on what you're fishing for; she also talks at length about breaking strain, pointing out that a line of one single hair is strong enough to catch a minnow but one of six hairs will be required for chub, bream, tench and eels.

1. *29 September and 2 February.*

15

The history of fish and chips

Like most success stories, the invention of this calorie-laden favourite is claimed by many people in many different countries. The sad news for the English, who traditionally parade this as a sort of national dish, is that chips were probably 'invented' in France or Belgium in the 17th century as an alternative to fish, which became scarce during harsh winters when the rivers froze over. Fried fish arrived in England courtesy of Portuguese Marranos (Jews who concealed their ethnicity for fear of persecution) and was originally served with bread or even a jacket potato.

Who first brought the two together? According to the National Federation of Fish Fryers, that honour belongs to one Joseph Malin who set up shop in 1860 in the East End of London and saw the birth of a business that took off as commercial fishing became more efficient and working people had more spare change in their pockets at the end of the week.

❛ To the deep despair of my parents, I went fishing. I resigned myself to being unsuccessful in life. ❜

Fishing Days, Geoffrey Bucknall

Barker's Delight or *The Art of Angling*

First published in 1651, *Barker's Delight* is a good barometer of the prevailing winds in angling at the time, combining as it does a love of fishing and a hearty appetite – indeed, nearly as much space is set aside to the preparing of the catch for the table as is given over to the actual catching.

As was common at the time, the author endorses a bewildering array of tackle and techniques, from fly fishing to ledgering lobworms for salmon, dapping flies for trout (though the author calls this 'dopping'), using a mix of blood and grain to attract carp and fishing a live minnow for perch. *Barker's Delight* also includes one of the first known references to snap tackle, a form of fishing for pike which involves two wired hooks which are used to secure a small live fish like a roach or dace; whilst this is deemed effective, his favourite method is to secure a goose or gander to the line and then set it loose in the hope that all the splashing about will attract a monster pike.

17

Species profile: The bream

Derided by some anglers as little more than a dead weight, loved by others for its habit of gathering in large shoals that feed freely, there's one thing that all fisherman can agree on. A net which has been used to land bream should not be left overnight in an enclosed space, for example the boot of a family car. The smell – nay, stench – of bream slime is eye-watering and will render the vehicle undrivable, even with all the windows open.

Good for: Steadily filling a keepnet.

'They overreach [outwit] the fish by an artful device. Round the hook they twist scarlet wool and two wings are secured on this wool from the feathers which grow under the wattles of a cock, brought up to the proper colour with wax. The rod they use is six feet in length and the line is of the same length. Then the angler lets fall his lure. The fish attracted by its colour, and excited, draws close, and judging from its beautiful appearance that it will obtain a marvellous banquet, forthwith opens its mouth but is caught by the hook, and bitter indeed is the feast it enjoys, inasmuch as it is captured.'

De Natura Animalium by Claudius Aelianus, describing the Macedonians fly-fishing for trout on the river Astaeus at the start of the 2nd century

Alien invasion – Top five threats to the UK's waters

1. The **American signal crayfish** is a beefed-up, pincer-snapping monstrosity; lady ASCs spread their favours far and wide, allowing their progeny to infest rivers, spreading disease and even collapsing the very banks they burrow into.

2. No friend to the water vole, bank shrew and moorhen, the **American mink** has no natural predators in the UK. Thumbs up to whoever let it in.

3. **Giant hogweed.** Can grow to 23 feet (7 metres) high. Toxic sap. Severe blistering. Long-term scarring. Blindness. Peter Gabriel-era Genesis wrote a song about it ('Kill them with your hogweed hairs/Heracleum mantigazziani'). Say no more.

4. **Floating pennywort** forms a buoyant 3ft (90cm) thick carpet that covers slow-moving rivers, blocking out the sun, starving them of oxygen and killing everything below. Except the American signal crayfish. Probably.

5. **Himalayan balsam**, the ultimate tease, produces loads of nectar so intoxicated bees don't pollinate other plants, chokes banks in summer, then dies off, leaving them bare and prone to erosion.

Izaak Walton: *The Compleat Angler,* 1653

No other character bestrides the world of coarse angling (see page 28) quite like Sir Izaak Walton, an ironmonger turned author who wrote *The Compleat Angler* which was first published in 1653. Originally 13 chapters long, the book is a leisurely stroll through various angling techniques interspersed with snatches of songs and poetry. Criticised by some for its lack of technical insight, this seems to rather miss the point of a book that was subtitled *The Contemplative Man's Recreation.* Walton fished and wrote for fun, and with the help of friends Charles Cotton and Thomas Barker[1] continued to revise and expand the original manuscript to include fly fishing and fly tying (which he readily admitted were beyond his expertise).

What's it like? In the main it's a discourse between 'Piscator' (fisherman) and 'Viator'[2] (wayfarer) as the first tries to persuade the second of the benefits of becoming a 'Brother of the Angle' – an occupation that the initially

---

1. See *Barker's Delight, page 17.*
2. This became 'Venator' (hunter) in later editions.

unconvinced Viator claims induces 'sorrow' in 'many grave, serious men'. The tone is friendly and playful, the facts fast and loose and the result is a marvellous combination of fact and – probably – fiction, mixed together like a fine groundbait to attract anglers, rather than fish. Take this description of the pike:

'All pikes that live long prove chargeable to their keepers because their life is maintained by the death of so many other fish, even those of his owne kind, which has made him by some writers to bee called the Tyrant of the Rivers, or the Freshwater-wolf, by reason of his bold, greedy, devouring disposition, which is so keen. As Gesner[1] relates, a man going to a Pond (where it seems a pike had devoured all the fish) to water his Mule, had a pike bit his mule by the lips, to which the pike hung so fast, that the Mule drew him out of the water, and by that accident the owner of the Mule got the Pike.'

1. Conrad Gesner, a Swiss physician and naturalist.

21

The coming of the railway

The boom in the railways coincided with a rise in wages for working families and a small increase in leisure time. It was now possible to escape the factory towns for a few hours at the weekend and fish in rivers and lakes where fish were plentiful. Fares were cheap and as the network spread, so did the opportunities to discover new waters.

Tom's day ticket

By the time Tom's awake, his father's been downstairs for 20 minutes and the house already feels alive again after the long, cold night. Dad's lit the fire and has got a brew on and when Tom walks into the kitchen, rubbing the sleep from his eyes, he's got his sleeves up and is kneading the remains of a stale loaf into bread paste. The muscles in his forearms flex and knot as he turns the bread into a smooth, elastic paste, soft enough for the fish to take, stiff enough to stay on the hook. Tom still has backache and some dirt under his fingernails from the hour spent last night pulling worms up from the lawn. They'd got loads. His dad ruffles his hair as he takes a cup of tea up to mum and Tom can smell the paste, clean and fragrant.

The street is empty apart from uncle Harry who's waiting for them under a street light, rolling a cigarette. Above him factory smoke still hangs in the air. The two men nod to each other and Harry hoists his bag onto a shoulder and picks up his rod. The three of them make their way down the hill to the railway station – their shadows, greatcoats, each with a bag and a rod, make them look like soldiers marching off to war.

The tickets only cost a few shillings[1] and by the time the station clock strikes 7.00 they're settled in their seats with dozens of other men and boys, coughing and farting and laughing, breathing hard on the window, drawing the

1. Until the 1960s fares were based on distance travelled and costed in old pence. Tom, his dad and uncle Harry would have paid one and a half pence a mile to travel 3rd class.

outlines of the giant fish they have yet to catch. By the time Tom sees the first glint of the distant river the carriages have settled, by the time the train pulls into the station everyone on board is standing, businesslike and ready. By the time the first float is cast into the smooth, glassy water, they are already in another world.

Angling gets organised

As industry took hold, so factories generated waste and looked around for ways to get rid of it easily and cheaply. Rivers were an obvious choice. Factories were often built on their banks and legislation to prevent them dumping whatever they liked was lax or nonexistent. Anglers and other water users were unable to protest effectively because they were disorganised and had no voice.

The history of the various – dozens? hundreds? – of angling bodies need not detain us here. Over the years, angling's attempts to organise itself have been dogged by infighting and finger-pointing, with alliances made, broken and remade in different forms. That

shouldn't detract from the very real advances that were made by groups like the National Federation of Anglers (founded in 1903, and which grew to be coarse fishing's largest national organisation) or the Anglers' Co-operative Association started by John Eastwood in 1948, one of the first angling-led organisations to take on polluters and help reaffirm the common-law rights of clean water.

These days, it's the turn of the Angling Trust to have a go.[1] Founded in 2009, it brought together all the remaining large angling bodies under one roof – coarse, game and sea – with the stated aim of promoting and protecting the rights of anglers.

And that concludes our scattergun look at angling through the ages. Horrendous gaps everywhere, we know – where's the history of the float, what about reels, or carp and monastic stewponds, and most important, when did angling split into coarse and game?

We're glad you asked. Pick up your tackle and we'll see you over the page.

1. The author's a member and suggests you check out the AT at www.anglingtrust.net

The death of Benson

When she was found dead in July 2009, Benson, a beautiful, fully scaled common carp who at her peak weighed a monstrous 64 lb (29 kg) sent the angling world into mourning. Even those who'd never tried for her were saddened at the thought that this enormous fish had succumbed to a handful of uncooked tiger nuts, used by some dopey angler who didn't know any better. And her name? It came from a distinctive hole in her dorsal fin that looked like a cigarette burn. She was originally one of a pair and yes, the other one was called Hedges.

Species profile: The bullhead

With its small body and large, flat head, the affable bullhead is a familiar sight to small children scooping nets in and out of clear streams. Able to perform chameleon-like camouflage tricks to blend in with the river bed, the males guard their partner's eggs jealously, oxygenating the water by flapping their tails vigorously.

Good for: A treat for net-fishing kids.

CHAPTER ONE

COARSE OR GAME?

Having dipped into a little of angling's chequered past and understood something of the historical and literary tides that have shaped it, we must now attempt to define and distinguish between its three main disciplines. Every angler reaches this point sooner or later, and although the decision to pursue one branch or another may be hard to quantify (intellectual rigour or a bit of emotional pin-the-tail-on-the-donkey?), it's as well to understand a bit about the relative attractions and pitfalls of each. Except maybe sea angling…

Coarse fishing in brief

In common with much to do with angling, the term 'coarse' fish came from the toffs. The typical 19th-century English gentleman who enjoyed fishing also enjoyed eating what he caught and it quickly became clear that trout and salmon were tastier than chub or roach – memorably described by some as having the texture of 'cotton wool and needles'.

These days 'coarse fishing' means fishing in fresh water – a pond, stream, river, drain, canal, lake or reservoir – for anything that isn't a trout or salmon; occasionally there's some confusion as to whether the grayling is a coarse fish or not but since they're relatively rare, it's not worth worrying about.[1]

There are coarse fishing techniques too – in fact, anything that isn't fishing with an artificial fly in fresh water is probably coarse fishing, which may also help illuminate the grayling conundrum. If not, how about this? If you catch a grayling on a fly it's a game fish, but if you catch it on a worm or a spinner, it's a coarse fish.

1. *It's actually a member of the salmon (Salmonidae) family.*

 28

Game fishing in brief

If you've read the previous page then this next bit is easy. Game fishing is the art (oh hell... deep water already) of catching a trout or salmon with an artificial fly – either one bought in a shop or one that you have tied yourself. On the face of it, this fly must look like the natural flies that the fish are taking at that moment in order to bring success, but every fly fisherman knows that the world is stranger than that, and every one of them has a tale of some desperate, unconvincing, badly tied, squint-eyed monster that looks more like a Muppet than a March Brown – yet turns out to be the only fly the fish will take on this or that afternoon.

This is not to get sidetracked into tactics or techniques – there'll be plenty of time for that later on – but to highlight the joyfully unpredictable nature of a style of fishing that prides itself on purity of purpose but which is also happy to muddy the metaphorical waters too, when it suits. Thus, sea trout anglers will use spinners to catch fish under certain conditions or when flies fail, and still call it game fishing.

29

A note on salmon fishing

Before leaving game fishing, let us salute the salmon angler, the salmon and their unlikely romance. We toast the angler for his dedication to this least predictable – and most hair-raisingly expensive – branch of the sport, and the salmon for fighting its way upstream through rapids, falls and deep, dangerous pools (surrounded by salmon anglers) in order to spawn.

Do either of them know what they're in for? The angler who may not catch – or even see – a single salmon in an entire season? The fish which – depending on whether it's a Pacific or Atlantic salmon – has between a zero and 10 per cent chance of making it back to the ocean alive? We think not.

No thanks, I'm not hungry

Perhaps the most peculiar aspect of salmon fishing is that when they reach fresh water, salmon stop feeding. Their stomachs shrink then whither away, and the space behind is used to make milt in the males and eggs in the hens. This means when they snap at a fly or a lure, they're not actually interested in eating it. As our friends in the US say – go figure.

How much? - The relative cost of tackle explored

The arrival of cheap fishing tackle of every description from China has reduced the cost of all forms of angling. Like most things cut from the cheapest cloth, there are real variations in value, with some rods and reels being comparable to established and expensive name brands, while others are shabbily made from substandard materials. If something that requires precision engineering is incredibly cheap – say a centrepin reel for £30 or less – treat it with suspicion.

That said, here's our rule of thumb. A salmon angler will spend more on their sport than a trout fisher, who will in turn spend more than a coarse angler. A couple of caveats to go with that: first, all forms of angling have premium or signature items that cost many times more than you'd normally pay; second, fishing tackle is big business and angling companies are past masters at selling you stuff that you don't need. Buy wisely at the beginning and you'll save money in the long run.

 31

Species profile: The carp

Brought here by monks in the 13th century who bred it in stewponds for food, the carp is the single most popular quarry for anglers in England (in the US it's often despised as a 'trash fish'). Originally deemed too hard to catch (Barnes describes the carp as 'an evil fish to take'[1]), the carp has swept all before it to become the single most sought-after fish that swims in the UK. It's spawned an entire industry both in terms of tackle and of managed lakes where large carp are encouraged at the expense of other species. From its place at the pinnacle of angling achievement, the carp has now fallen to the extent that it's now the first fish that many anglers catch.

There are two kinds of carp. Little ones (crucian carp, round, dainty, with large, surprised eyes and scales like burnished gold) and big ones (all the rest). Usually anglers will catch common and mirror carp, sometimes leather and linear carp, less often grass and ornamental carp and finally, rarest of all, true wild carp, the slim, powerful descendants of those fish brought here by the fish-loving friars. A typical carp will weigh between 5 and 15 lb (6.8 kg); a big one is 20 lb (9 kg) or more, and any fish on the far side of 30 lb (13.5 kg) is a monster. The current British record stands at 67 lb 14 oz (30 kg). Strewth.

Good for: A wise old carp can live for 40 years, which makes them worthy opponents.

1. in A treatyse of fysshynge wyth an Angle.

The fish themselves

The traditional view of salmon as noble, trout as cunning and everything else as just coarse, ignores the facts. As they near the spawning grounds, many salmon develop an ugly hook to their jaws and a raw, red look. Some grow humps. While our native brown trout may be adept at avoiding anglers, the rainbow trout, introduced here from the US in the 1880s, is much more of an open-all-hours fish and can be caught by almost anyone on almost any tackle. Coarse fishermen routinely catch them by accident. By contrast, many coarse fish – like the barbel, dace and crucian carp – are hard to catch and incredibly beautiful.

The fishing club

Fishing clubs are a good idea. They allow individual anglers to gather in groups (should that be shoals?) where everyone pays a small annual fee and the money is used to convince riparian and land owners to lease them access to whatever water is on their property. Clubs usually take on the upkeep of the water, banks, access, parking and so on, and often clear

33

spaces where anglers sit to fish – called swims; they may even construct platforms that poke out over the water that allow the angler to perch at the end like a portly heron going about its business.

While most anglers like their sport to come with the minimum number of rules and regulations, the people who run clubs often get tangled up in the mechanics of the thing or become overzealous, tidying away banks until they have a manicured Capability Brown look.

The angling syndicate

You'll likely know there's a difference between a club and a syndicate without even being told. Clubs sound small and friendly, syndicates sound serious; clubs are welcoming, syndicates have more of a come-on-in-if-you-think-you're-hard-enough feel to them; clubs are inexpensive and usually provide access to a number of different waters, while syndicates are costly and may only offer a single, more specialised water – often one that contains large carp, pike or catfish.

If you can afford it, syndicates have real advantages. Fewer members means less pressure on the water and more chance of getting the place to yourself; and some of these fisheries hold enormous specimens, the like of which many anglers will never see. And while a club may advertise locally for members, a syndicate rarely needs to and will quietly, secretly turn over a member or two every year, usually by word of mouth. Shhhhhh…

About the adipose fin

This is the fishy equivalent of the appendix because although we know it exists – look, it's over there between the dorsal and the caudal (or tail) fins – nobody knows what it does. Scientists who've cut the adipose fin from some fish have noticed that their tails beat faster as a result – probably in an attempt to get away from whatever's cutting their fins off. Trout, salmon and grayling all have adipose fins.

The angler's attire

If clothes maketh the man, what are we then to make of the typical angler? Here comes a group of them now, one after the other, not speaking but clearly excited at the thought of the day's sport to come. The first is dressed in old-fashioned gear, tweed jacket with patched leather elbows, moleskin trousers and galoshes. The next comes head to foot in camouflage and carries a huge pack riding high on his back as if he's just stepped off a Hercules; the third is in tough coveralls, emblazoned with various brand names and wearing sturdy D.I.Y-store wellington boots. After that comes one in shorts and T-shirt, flip-flops, neck blazing red and angry in the sun, and finally, trailing along a pace or two back is one who looks like he may have spent the night asleep in someone's allotment – mismatched socks, patched jeans, an ancient shirt, sleeves rolled up, the quilted inside of a winter coat as a waistcoat and a baseball cap with 'Fairport Convention' written on it.

It's like the Ascent of Man, only in reverse.

Beverages

Anglers nearly always need a drink. They need one when they arrive at the water in order to get going. They need one when the fish have vanished – again – and there's nothing left to do, and they need one to keep warm on a cold, winter's afternoon. They need one to toast their successes – this is best done with a friend – and one to take the edge off their failures, biliously and alone.

The weapon of choice? Tea or instant coffee for general coarse fishermen, often with plenty of sugar, coffee for carp and pike anglers – the strong, ground stuff – unless they're over-nighting in a bivvy,[1] in which case it's beer. Energy drinks for pole anglers – even if all that caffeine makes the pole quiver. Do fly anglers invariably drink chilled white wine or a nip from a hip flask and do salmon fishers take a glass of single malt as required, while staring purposefully up the glen?

Who knows? Ours is a cup of builder's tea with more milk than you think, thanks very much.

1. A small, one-person tent.

 37

Types of water

Apparently, you cannot step in the same river twice,[1] and any angler knows that each time you approach the water you're likely to find something different. Different types of water, though, do have certain characteristics.

The pond – Good for beginners. They have several advantages over other types of water. They're still, on the whole (though if they're stream-fed there may be a gentle current where the flow enters the pond), which is enormously helpful for novices because their tackle – float or ledger – doesn't move about. It's also easier to find the fish in a small pond and easier to get at them because you don't have to cast as far.

Good for: Catching roach, rudd, small carp, skimmer bream, tench, perch and maybe a pike.

The stream – On slow-moving streams you can drop a float into the water in front of you and let it drift – or 'trot' – down with the current. Fast streams are more of a challenge

---

1. *Heraclitus, sometimes called the 'weeping philosopher', said this. Maybe he was an angler.*

38

because the current wants to pull your float or ledger round in an arc so it ends up under your own bank, further downstream. (Note: larger fish like to tuck in under banks, out of the current, so it's also a good place to try.) It's also harder to control and to see a fly on fast, rippling water.

Good for: Dace, chub, trout, gudgeon, roach, perch and pike; maybe even a barbel or grayling.

Species profile: The barbel

Considered by many as the hardest-fighting fish, pound-for-pound, in UK waters, the barbel is an aristocrat among river fish and one of the few coarse fish that actually *looks* intelligent, as if it were somehow sizing you up. A powerful, bottom-hugging, triangular body, large fins and plenty of determination make the barbel a tough, tough opponent.

Good for: Scaring the bejaysus out of the unwary chub angler.

The lake – Here the challenge is to find the features that turn fish on. So, they like to rummage around the roots of reed beds looking for snails, bloodworm and other tasty morsels and they patrol the edges of lakes – called the margins – doing the same thing. All fish like gravel bars because they sit in shallower water, warm up in the sun more quickly and 'catch' food blown across the lake by the wind. Although many good fish can be caught under your rod tip, you may need to fish at a distance and tackle – particularly a float – is harder to control.

Good for: Same stuff that's in a pond but bigger.

The river – Big rivers are monsters. Hard to control your tackle in all that flow, line bites galore in autumn (debris drifting down the river hits your line and can feel like a fish tugging) and the fish could be anywhere. While there'll be some obvious fish-holding features – gravel bars, deep holes, undercut banks, fallen trees and so on – rivers change all the time, from season to season and from year to year. Broadly speaking, they'll follow the riffle-pool sequence of shallower stretches

interspersed with deeper pools. You can recognise these by looking at the surface – pools are smooth and glassy, riffles are everything else. If in doubt, fish the top or bottom edge of a pool in summer and the pool itself in the winter.

Good for: Same stuff that's in a stream but bigger; may also catch sea trout if there's a run.

The Christmas carp

Were you to prepare a carp for Christmas dinner (and we really, really wouldn't), this is how to do it:

Gut and clean the fish thoroughly and remove the head. Poach for 30 minutes in a fish and vegetable stock. Pour the stock off into a jug and clarify with the white of an egg mixed with a little dissolved gelatin. Let the fish cool and then pour the mixture over it. Decorate with slices of carrot and hard-boiled eggs and leave until set.[1]

1. *Don't do any of this, just put it back.*

The work party

Three or four times a year, groups of – usually – unconfident, overweight and ill-equipped anglers will gather together by a lake or river without their fishing tackle. Stripped of the props associated with angling they will mill about until someone (often the club secretary) arrives and starts dishing out jobs. Those with waders will be dispatched into the margins to clear weed and dead rushes anyone with sailing experience (yes, pedalos count) may find themselves in a rickety boat that smells of maggots, pulling up handfuls of lily pads in order to clear more space; the rest will be sent down the banks to cut down stinging nettles, Himalayan balsam and anything else that prevents a fully laden angler from wobbling down to the water's edge.

Individually, the key is to look busy so you don't get anything too onerous to do; collectively, it's important to strike a balance between tidying up (which is good) and tidying away (which is too much like gardening for our liking). Before you ask, no, you won't get paid (you may not even get any thanks) but yes, if you check the rule book you may see that attending at least one work party a year is a condition of membership. Just don't forget your Marigolds.

How to stuff a fish

If you must do this, wear those Marigolds and open all the windows...

Cut along the lateral line and separate the skin from the flesh with a filleting knife, all the way round so what you're left with is the head and tail joined by the skin – it should look a bit like an open sports bag. Clean out as much of the meat as you can and then inject formalin directly into any parts you can't clean out. Sprinkle a layer of borax onto all the inside surfaces and rub it in. Use needle and thread to stitch the fish about halfway up its body, leaving about half an inch (13 mm) between stitches, then pack with sawdust and tamp down with a stick; keep packing, then finish stitching up. Shape the fish, then clean off with a brush and damp sponge. Put mounting card behind the fins and pin them in the required position, then put some fibreglass wool into the eye socket and then add the false eye. Leave to dry for at least a month, then paint and varnish.

> **❛** I have peeped behind the veil of the taxidermist's craft, and what I saw amazed me. **❜**

Angling Ways, E. Marshall Hardy

The angler's transport

In the main, anglers travel by car, usually because their destination is too far to get to otherwise, or too off the beaten track. Carry less gear (you'll hear us bang this particular drum again) and it may be possible to use public transport or even cycle, like you might have done when you were a kid. Few of us are lucky enough to live close to anywhere worth fishing that's in walking distance but if you do, then you are twice blessed. Once because you're going fishing and twice because that's also your exercise for the day.

Why aren't whales fish, again?

Because they're mammals that give birth to live young, rather than laying eggs, and have to surface periodically to breathe – every 20 minutes or so if they're little fin whales, every 90 minutes for the altogether larger sperm whales. But we prefer to identify whales as mammals because – like dolphins – their tails move up and down, rather than from side to side. Close your eyes and think about them moving the other way... Ew, that'd be just wrong.

Species profile: The catfish

They like deep, warm water and are equally at home in lakes or slow-flowing rivers like the mighty Ebro in Spain. With their long, whiskery barbules they resemble cats (if you think that cats look like giant used condoms) and are voracious feeders, occasionally rising to take ducks off the surface.

Good for: Being on your side in a fight with a shark (especially the giant Mekong catfish).

Recipe: Pan-fried catfish

Use thin fillets, less than ¼" (6 mm) thick, rinse them under cold running water and dry. Lay them in a dish and cover with milk – leave for 10 minutes. Meanwhile, combine one cup of cornmeal, two teaspoons of salt, one of black pepper and one of cayenne pepper in a second dish. Dip the fillets in the mixture, making sure they're evenly coated, then heat the oil in a large frying pan and when it's good and hot, cook for 7 minutes each side until golden brown.

Sea angling

Any sea anglers among you are to be congratulated on getting this far with so little encouragement and may have been drawn to these pages in the belief that your moment has arrived. Cruelly however, the disappointment is set to continue. This branch of the sport is so vast and so strange to those of us who ply our trade on inland waters that we're going to give a nod only in its direction and then move on.

It could simply be that we've never quite forgiven the unscrupulous tackle dealer who sold us our first rod while on holiday in Cornwall. Despite making it clear that our local fishery was a half-acre pond in Bucks, we still walked out of his shop with a two-piece, six-foot boat rod with a handle made of solid wood, which we stuck with until our pocket money accumulated enough to buy a replacement – about a year and a half later.

Or it could be that our one boat trip ended in miserable failure where the only thing we managed to hook – while the rest of the boat gleefully pulled in mackerel after mackerel –

was the tackle of an angler on the other side of the boat who, being much larger than we were, nearly pulled us in.

Anyway, sea fishing's great. It's free, there are loads of different places to have a go – rocks, beaches, breakwaters, piers, estuaries, harbours or off a boat over a wreck (sea fish love wrecks). The tackle's like freshwater tackle except bigger, heavier and stronger. And you can usually eat what you catch[1] – unless it's a stingray or a greater or lesser weaver.

OK, we've touched briefly on different types of fishing and what you might expect when you try them out, so now it's time for a visit to the place where anglers go to worship – the tackle shop – to look at some of the tools of the trade.

1. www.fishonline.org has a list of sustainable seafood.

❝ The pike is said to eat twice his weight of food every week; a ten pounder thus demolishes 520 pounds of fish in the year. ❞

Super Flumina, Charles Latimer Marson

❝ ...without undue conceit, I have noticed one thing, namely, that whereas many other fishermen exceed me in skill, nevertheless I have been gifted with the capacity of catching fish. ❞

Fish, Lord Walsingham

CHAPTER TWO

TACKLE

There's a school of thought that says (persuasively to our minds) that fishing tackle is mainly designed to catch anglers, not fish. Thus, rods and reels carry labels like Assassin, Dominator, Technium or our favourite, Avocet (perfectly designed to attract the passing angler, this – a wading bird that sounds like a missile). Still, there's no escaping the fact that every angler needs some tackle[1] so let's examine the basics – rods, reels and a bit of what goes on the end.

---

1. Or maybe not – see 'Tickling trout', p. 53.

The rod, the reel and the end tackle

Anyone who's ever used a hand line will appreciate the sheer physics of a rod and reel. It allows you to cast much further, control the float, ledger or lure more effectively; the rod's 'action' (essentially the shape of the bend when you've got something on the other end) removes much of the strain from the line and the reel itself can be set to release the line to a fighting fish, before it snaps under the strain. Rods come in different lengths but for general purpose coarse fishing, 12 or 13 ft (3.6–3.9 m) is the most useful, matched with a fixed-spool reel (see page 59). For fly fishing, choose a rod not less than 8 ft (2.4 m) but no more than 10 ft (3 m) with a small, centrepin-style fly reel.

At the business end coarse anglers will need a way of casting and presenting the bait, either using a float balanced with small weights pinched onto the line or a weight called a ledger which sinks the bait to the bottom. Fly fishing's a whole different thing – a bit like voodoo – where the line itself provides the weight for casting (see pages 101–102).

The beginner's basic kit

No matter what your poison, you'll need a rod, a reel and some line. At the other end of the line you'll need a hook and something to make the fish swallow it – either by making the hook look like a fly, a small fish or a worm, an insect, slug or frog, or by using bait that they like to eat, like maggots, bread, corn, worm and so on. A few floats, some ledger weights or some flies, and you're done.

If you're float fishing or fly fishing, you'll know when you've got a bite – the float will dip and disappear and the fly will get swallowed – but if you're fishing with a weight on the bottom (ledgering) you may also need an electronic alarm which senses when a fish takes the bait and starts to take line from the reel. In that case you'll also need rests for your rod to keep it steady while you're waiting for a bite. You may also need something to sit on and – if the weather is inclement – sit under. Then you might like something hot to drink. For years our most expensive piece of equipment was a flask.

Parts of a fishing rod

All fishing rods are made from three components – the butt or handle, the rod itself and the rings. Rod butts are often made from cork or that funny man-made stuff that feels a bit like velvet; they also have two rings (or a proper threaded 'seat') where you attach the reel. Fly-rod butts are short and the reel goes at the back. Coarse-rod butts are longer and the reel is seated towards the front.

These days most rods are made from carbon fibre which makes them light, flexible and strong. They come in sections that fit together (if they didn't you'd never get them in the car); usually two or three, but sometimes more for very long rods, or travel rods which are designed to fit inside rugged, portable tubes.

Rings are whipped onto the rod at different intervals – further apart near the butt, closer together nearer the tip; the line passes through the rings and they should be checked regularly for wear and tear.

Tickling trout

The grass is wet and cold as he inches towards the water's edge and the stream that chuckles beyond it, just out of sight. Off in the distance the farmer's big, ugly old dogs bark once, twice and then set off in a cacophony of growls and whines and whoops. One sleeve rolled up, he inches his arm into the icy water, palm down, fingers curled towards the bank. Then he waits. He waits for the silky touch of a trout's flaccid stomach to flutter against the tips of his fingers. Time passes and as night gathers around him he waits for the trout to come.

Let coarse bold hands from slimy nest
The bedded fish in banks out-wrest;
Or curious traitors, sleave-silk flies,
Bewitch poor fishes' wand'ring eyes.

For thee, thou need'st no such deceit,
For thou thyself art thine own bait:
That fish, that is not catch'd thereby,
Alas, is wiser far than I.

The Baite, John Donne

The Avon/quiver rod

If we had to recommend a single rod for general-purpose coarse fishing it would be this – the Avon/quiver rod. Typically a two-section rod between 11 and 12 ft (3.3–3.5 m) long, it's designed for both float fishing and ledgering. How so? Well, when you open the bag you'll find a bottom rod section and two entirely separate top sections – so that's three bits of rod for your money.

The first top looks like the bottom section – same colour, same stiffish action – and is designed for float fishing and using heavier ledgers. The second top has a slimmer, lighter tip that's also brightly coloured to make it easier to see. This is called a quiver tip and is used for lighter ledgering where it's excellent at showing delicate finicky bites – a bite will pull the tip round. Matched with a fixed spool reel and line of between 3 and 7 lb (1.3–3.2 kg) breaking strain, this single rod will handle all of the fish that a typical pleasure angler will hook – with the exception of large pike, carp and salmon. And even then it'll give them a good run for their money.

feeder rod

Feeder rods take their name from swimfeeders, clever little cages the size of a cotton reel that are attached to the line down near the hook end and packed with bait and groundbait that's designed to trickle out through the holes in the cage to attract fish to the hook. Feeder rods are usually between 11 and 13 ft (3.3–3.9 m) and need to be balanced to the size of feeder they're casting. So, big swimfeeder, big rod.

Poles

Poles are very long rods without reels, so you don't cast as such. Instead, the line (which may only be a few yards or metres long) is attached to the end of the pole via some elastic. To 'cast' you add another section to the pole, then another and then another, pushing it out over the water until it's at the required distance. Then you drop the tackle – always a little float – into the water. Pole fishing is a very precise way of catching fish but is also a bit of a palaver and requires more space and more gear. Match anglers love poles.

fly rods

Once only the preserve of those with deep pockets, it's now possible to buy a good little fly rod for £50 or less. The trick is to start with the line you're going to fish with and then match the rod to that. Although there's a huge range to choose from (and fly fishing's numbering systems are bamboozling for beginners) if you go with a 5-line weight and an 8 ft 6 inch (2.5 m) rod, you won't be far off for general-purpose fishing.

'First, let your rod be light, and very gentle; I take the best to be of two pieces: and let not your line exceed (especially for three or four links next to the hook) I say, not exceed three or four hairs at the most, though you may fish a little stronger above, in the upper part of your line; but if you can attain to angle with one hair, you shall have more rises and catch more fish.'

The Compleat Angler, Izaak Walton

five household items
you can use for tackle

1. **Bite indicator** – tin foil folded into a rectangle, then bent in half over the line.

2. **Float** – a matchstick

3. **Artificial bait** – cut up bits of yellow bath sponge to look like sweetcorn.

4. **Bead punch** – use the tube from a cheap biro, press into soft bread, blow down other end to propel it into hand.

5. **Bite alarm** – use the spring bell from a budgerigar's cage attached to a hairgrip; pull a length of the line from between the reel and the first ring and thread it through the hairgrip – when a fish pulls the line, the bell will ring.

Species profile: The char

A kind of cross between a salmon and a trout, the Arctic char (to give it its full name) is one of Britain's rarest fish. Originally from the seas off Iceland, it migrated south and then, when the last ice age struck, got stranded there. Found in deep, glacial lakes where the cold would kill other fish. If you're lucky enough to catch one, prepare for a fight.

Good for: Add a dab of dill butter. They taste like salmon.

Carp and pike rods

Purists would separate these two but we've always found that what's good for a pike is good for a carp and vice versa. Stick to about 12 ft (3.6 m) with a test curve of between 2 and 4 lb (0.9–1.8 kg) and you'll have a rod that'll handle casting some distance but is sensitive enough to make fishing close in fun as well. We prefer a slightly stiffer action on these rods because it makes casting heavy weights less unpredictable.

Reels

Unless you're fishing with a pole, you'll need a reel. There are four types:

- **The old-fashioned centrepin**, which is essentially a freewheeling spool on an axle.

- **The fixed-spool reel** reduces this in size, makes it deeper, turns it 90 degrees, stops it from rotating (hence the 'fixed' spool) and then wraps the line onto it courtesy of an ingenious rotating bale arm.

- **The multiplier** is like a fat centrepin with gears, so that each turn of the handle rotates the spool more than once.

- **The fly reel** – a tiny centrepin and little more than a spool for storing the line. In coarse fishing the rod and reel work together to play the fish, but in fly fishing the rod does all the hard work.

Fixed-spool reels are far and away the most popular and start from about £10 or £15; they're reliable, easy to use and handle nearly every style of fishing – with the possible exception of trotting – really well.

fishing lines

There are hundreds of different coarse fishing lines – thin or supple, stretchy and not, some that don't have any 'memory' so they coil and uncoil from the reel more smoothly, some that use refraction to disappear when they're in the water, and so on.

Line comes in different breaking strains – 4 lb (1.8 kg) line will snap when you exert much more than 4 lb of pressure on it – and you should match this to the size of fish you're after. Fly lines are a bit different. You need less – maybe 25–35 yards (23–32 m) – and it's attached to a thinner backing line which bulks out the spool (so the fly line doesn't twist and turn so much) and also lets you play a fish that takes a lot of line. It's made from a core of braid or nylon, is coated with PVC and comes in floating or sinking varieties. Remember that the line weight must match that of your rod – so use a 7 line with a 7 rod and so on. At the business end you'll need a finer section of line called a leader or tippet onto which you tie the fly.

floats

Floats come in thousands of different shapes and sizes but they all do the same job – allowing you to position and control the line, weights, hook and bait beneath them, and indicating when you've got a bite. With the addition of a tube and a little glow-in-the-dark chemical light, you can even use them at night.

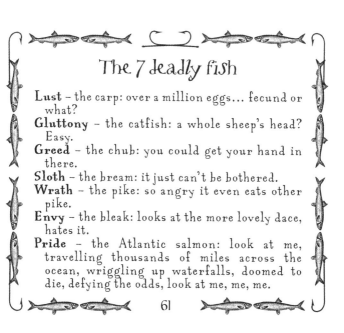

The 7 deadly fish

Lust – the carp: over a million eggs… fecund or what?

Gluttony – the catfish: a whole sheep's head? Easy.

Greed – the chub: you could get your hand in there.

Sloth – the bream: it just can't be bothered.

Wrath – the pike: so angry it even eats other pike.

Envy – the bleak: looks at the more lovely dace, hates it.

Pride – the Atlantic salmon: look at me, travelling thousands of miles across the ocean, wriggling up waterfalls, doomed to die, defying the odds, look at me, me, me.

61

Ledgers and feeders

Ledgers are weights. They're attached to the line in various ways, usually so it can be pulled through them in either direction. In this way, when a fish takes the bait, it can pull the line without feeling any resistance from the weight and you can see the end of the rod knocking or watch the line being drawn from the reel. Some ledgers aren't free-running at all. The idea here is that the fish takes the bait, feels the weight, panics and then hooks itself as it tries to scarper. Such weights are usually heavier as well.

A feeder is a cage attached to a weight. It might be a literal cage or a plastic container with round holes bored into it. The idea here is that you fill the feeder with something to attract the fish – either groundbait or samples of what's on the hook – and that this escapes through the holes to carpet the area where you're fishing. Feeders can be free-running or fixed, like ledgers.

Bait boats

Sometimes the fish won't co-operate and instead stick doggedly to a particular part of the lake, right over the other side, under the trees where you can't get at them. The answer is a small radio-controlled boat. Pop your baited hook and end tackle onto the boat along with a selection of free offerings, guide it to the other side of the lake, then flick a switch and the deck of the boat either flips up or opens down to deposit the whole lot into the water in exactly the right spot.[1]

Species profile: The chub

Native to rivers but also stocked in some still waters, the chub is an obliging fish, willing to feed on even freezing days, and give you a good scrap thanks to large spade-like fins. Handsome rather than pretty, chub grow to over 8 lb (3.6 kg) and fish of around 3 lb (1.3 kg) are common enough. You can ledger or float-fish for chub and even take them on a fly.

Good for: Warming the heart of an angler on a cold day.

1. *This may be ingenious but it's also cheating.*

Hooks and knots

As with line, tackle makers work hard to convince you that there's a difference between the hundreds of different hooks on the market. Essentially you need small hooks for small baits and fish up to 3 or 4 lb (1.3–1.8 kg) and bigger hooks for bigger baits and larger fish. We could argue the toss as to whether mechanical or chemical sharpening is best or if round bends are more effective than crystal bends, but instead we'll just say this: don't buy the cheapest hooks, and always buy barbless – they're kinder to the fish and better for your karma.

Entire books have been written about anglers' knots and we're not going to compete in a few sentences... Oh, go on, then. Practise on string first because it's easier than monofilament. When you come to tie real knots, moisten them with a bit of spit before pulling tight, use nail clippers to trim off any excess when you're done. Always check the last 6 ft (1.8 m) or so of line for kinks and abrasions before starting.

64

Places you must fish

Everyone has a favourite fishing spot. Ours is a stretch of a small river so unremarkable that most people wouldn't give it a second thought; but for us it is a place full of resonance and powerful memories. So we offer this list on the understanding that your list may be entirely different.

For salmon, the rivers Tay and Tweed in Scotland and the Tamar in Devon and Cornwall; for trout, the rivers Test and Itchen in the south of England; for barbel, the river Wye on the Welsh borders and the Buckinghamshire Ouse; for roach, the river Test and the Dorset Stour; for Tench (quick, while they're still there), Blenheim Palace lake in Oxfordshire. Try any small commercial fishery for perch – most anglers fish these for carp and there are plenty of small fish for the perch to gorge on. For pike, go north to Loch Awe. For rudd, try Twetifield fishery next to the M6. And for gudgeon – why not? – Old Father Thames.

Some extras

By now you know how we feel about tackle, but if you must continue to fill the pockets of the manufacturers, here's what we'd recommend.

- **Landing net** – big enough to cope with what you're fishing for and with a handle long enough to stretch down a high bank if needed.

- **Rod rests** – we use little extendable ones that fit in a small bag; you can get big ones too.

- **Polarised glasses** – these cut out surface glare and let you see what's going on under the water more clearly.

- **Something to sit on** – we use an inflatable cushion but watching us get up isn't a pretty sight; if you're getting a chair, get a light one with individually adjustable wide-bottomed feet.

- **Something to keep you dry** – a poncho for roving, an umbrella for sitting down.

Species profile: The dace

Imagine a miniature chub but with a concave anal fin instead of a convex one. Only grows to just over a pound, loves fast rivers and anglers with slow reactions. Try trotting for them with a long rod and centrepin and casters. And good luck hitting those lightning bites.

Good for: Measuring your reaction times.

As we're at the tackle-shop door, laden down with a new rod, reel, line and several 'must-have' extras, there's a little tug at our sleeves. Turning round, we're greeted by the sight of the smiling shop owner who's holding out a veritable banquet of things that squirm, stuff that smells of curry and strawberries (at the same time) and tiny things that look like earrings and brooches.

With a sigh we turn and follow him back into the shop.

> Hops and turkeys, carps and beer
> Came into England all in a year.

Sir Richard Baker,
*Chronicle of the Kings of England from
the Time of the Romans' Government unto
the Death of King James*, 1643

> The salmon that idles its
> way downstream will never
> leap the waterfall.

The footballer Eric Cantona announces his
intention to leave Leeds United by fax to
his agent Jean-Jacques Bertrand.

CHAPTER THREE

BAITS, LURES AND FLIES

Once, when fishing in Thailand with a small spinner, we returned from another unsuccessful trip to hoots and guffaws from the waiters at the beach bar. They'd seen the little silver spoon on the end of our line and the tiny treble hook, but couldn't believe we weren't also using bait.

'Where your bait?' they shouted, beside themselves with mirth, 'Thai fish not stupid, Mr. Lob!' Looking at our empty bucket, maybe they had a point.

Nasty baits

Believe it or not, plenty of anglers are squeamish, which is something of a drawback – after all, it's hard to put something on a hook when you don't want to touch it. Everyone has their no-go areas (slugs for us, mainly because the slime is like glue and almost impossible to get rid of – try getting it off a car steering wheel) but with practice and a little grit, you can usually overcome most aversions.[1]

When you think about it, the hill isn't that big a one to climb, being mainly made up of maggots, casters (the pupae that a maggot turns into before becoming a fly), bloodworms, redworms, lobworms, dendrabenas (a kind of middling worm), slugs, cockles, prawns, shrimps, crayfish (good bait for chub, apparently, but we can never negotiate the eyes, antennae and waving claws… aaargh, run away). Non-fishing partners are surprisingly sensitive about all this stuff and if you return, flushed from a successful trip, and find your romantic advances rebuffed, invest in some strong-smelling soap.

1. Except slugs.

70

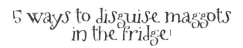

5 ways to disguise maggots in the fridge[1]

1. Buy unpopular frozen veg. Open bag. Throw veg away, half-fill with maggots. Seal bag with freezer clip. Put in bottom of freezer. Cross fingers.

2. Put in opaque plastic container. Cover with thick layer of oats (to absorb maggot sweat). Touch wood.

3. Always flavour maggots with strawberry essence (but if partner loves strawberries, change flavouring accordingly). Fondle lucky rabbit's foot.

4. Cultivate a liking for strong, blue cheese. Leave open in fridge – but away from maggots, obviously. Find four-leaf clover.

5. Place red and white maggots in large bag labelled 'pilau rice' in full view. Steal partner's glasses. Pray.

1. Note, all methods require chutzpah; none are guaranteed.

Slugs, grasshoppers and moths

'And when your worms, especially the brandling, begins to be sick and lose of his bigness, then you may recover him, by putting a little milk or cream, about a spoonful in a day, into them, by drops on the moss; and if there be added to the cream an egg beaten and boiled in it, then it will both fatten and preserve them long.'[1]

The Compleat Angler, Izaak Walton

Before everyone became obsessed with distance and the fashion became always to fish on the opposite side of the lake or river to where you're sitting, people used to fish under their own banks or in the margins. For fish like chub or carp who love to take food off the surface, there are few more effective baits than a free-lined[2] moth or grasshopper; while in rivers, the free-lined slug is like aphrodisiac for big chub.

1. *Mmmm, worm omelette…*
2. *i.e. just the line and the hook.*

Species profile: The eel

Ah, eels, with their huge, mad eyes, their mysterious breeding habits (they go to the Sargasso Sea to get it on but no one's ever actually caught them in the act) and ability to slither over wet fields when no one's looking. Fierce fighters, good eating (you can peel the skin off like removing a pair of tights from someone's leg), eels are voracious, particularly in the spring and summer when they'll eat virtually anything. A friend of ours caught one on a fly once.

Good for: Pretending you've got something else on the line.

Nice baits

Anyone who's spent the day digging through a mess of sweaty maggots on the turn or dipping into a bait box full of old, sour casters, always appreciates the chance to use a bait that doesn't make them want to throw up. Our definition here is broad, but essentially it's anything we wouldn't mind eating – or at least, taking a good, deep smell of.

Bread's a great bait. Versatile (you can make it into a paste that sinks, pinch it onto the hook as flake, use the crust that floats), it's cheap, freezes well, is visible in low light or murky water; and it's fragrant, especially the really cheap, nasty, white stuff. Same goes for cheese, only more so. We prefer using real cheese for paste rather than flavouring, and find that a mix of strong Cheddar and blue cheese has a strong aroma.

Sweetcorn is a fantastic bait. Convenient (either frozen or canned), colourful, easy to hook, doesn't need any preparation, easy to flavour and colour if you're that way inclined, and makes good loose feed for attracting fish to your swim. Although no longer seen as a wonder bait, luncheon meat (bacon grill, spam) will catch a lot more species than carp and chub, and we've caught many tench, roach, rudd and perch using it. Always tear a corner off the hookbait to release the smell and oils into the water.

You can catch carp using bananas (though they're a bugger to keep on the hook) and various kinds of berries and nuts; and carp love

dog biscuits fished on the surface – just make sure they're soft enough first by putting them in a plastic bag, adding a little hot water, then sealing the bag. By the time you get to the water they'll be ready.

Izaak Walton's paste recipe

'Take the flesh of a rabbit, or cat, cut small; and bean-flour; and if that may not be easily got, get other flour; and then, mix these together, and put to them either sugar, or honey, which I think better; and then beat these together in a mortar, or sometimes work them in your hands, your hands being very clean; and then make it into a ball, or two, or three, as you like best...'

The Compleat Angler, Izaak Walton

New baits

Modern techno-baits don't mess about and they don't take anything for granted. They're made, not by people like us, in shirtsleeves, standing at a sink and listening to the wireless, but by people in white coats who know their low-fat oceanic proteins from their N-butyric acid – and which ratios to use them in.

So let's have a big hand for all the proteins, enzymes, lecithins, mineral salts, trace elements, polysaccharides, attractor incitants, base mixes, balanced profiles, chemoreception and amino acid delivery systems. Where would fishing be without them?

Far from just finding a feeding fish and then trying to drop a bait in front of it, or carefully groundbaiting an area with natural offerings in the hope of encouraging fish to move in and start feeding, these baits are designed to pull fish into your swim like a magnet and then get them feeding – even if they aren't actually hungry.

Serious carp anglers often make their own baits using commercially bought base mixes (you can buy these in 20 kg sacks – why mess about?) and then adding various oils and flavourings – garlic strawberries, mmmm. The resulting mixture is turned into small, round hookbaits called 'boilies' which look rather like gobstoppers. In fact, they've got quite a lot in common with sweets; fish find them hypnotically attractive, and will wolf them down even when they're not especially hungry. These and other man-made baits will produce the kind of pot-bellied carp that have become commonplace in the pages of the angling press.

Can't be bothered? There are plenty of shop-bought boilies to try as well as a wide range of pellets of the kind used in fish farms to get the fish to put on weight quickly.

Make your own boilie

Although you can make your own base mix, that's a bit like mad science to us. Instead, try one that's a 50/50 balanced protein base mix and then visit the tackle shop and browse through their flavourings, sweeteners and colourings; add these to the mix following the instructions. These flavourings are really powerful so don't be tempted to put a little extra in. Alternatively, try supermarket flavourings like curry powder, garlic powder, fenugreek and soy sauce.

Start with 1 lb (0.45 kg) of mix. Beat four eggs in a bowl and then add the dry mix. Beat it thoroughly with a wooden spoon until it makes a sticky paste. Leave it for about 10 minutes. It'll harden slightly. Knead it by hand until it becomes a smooth mixture with plenty of give that doesn't stick to your fingers. Cut the paste up, roll it out into skinny sausages and then cut these into sections with a knife. Roll each section into a neat ball. Pop the finished balls into boiling water for between one and two minutes each, then scoop them out and leave to air-dry before popping them into bags. Boilies freeze quite happily for later.

Gudgeon-fishing parties

In the 19th century it was not unusual to see ladies and gentlemen take to their punts to fish for gudgeon. First, shallow gravel runs were raked to stir up the bottom, loosing larvae and other insects into the water to attract the voracious gudgeon. These were caught – usually by fishing a single red worm – and then fried up on the river bank as part of a jolly picnic.

'Give me mine angle; we'll to the river: there,
My music playing far off, I will betray
Tawny-finn'd fishes; my bended hook shall pierce
Their slimy jaws; and, as I draw them up,
I'll think them every one an Antony,
And say "Ah, ha! you're caught."'

William Shakespeare,
Antony and Cleopatra, 2.5

Lures, spinners & plugs

Predators like pike tend not to eat bread paste – so the best way to catch them is with something that mimics the movement of a small, preferably sickly fish. That's where lures, spinners and plugs come in.

For our purposes, lures are short lengths of undulating, burnished metal with a swivel at one end (which you tie to the line or a length of wire called a trace) and a treble hook at the other; as a lure is reeled in it wobbles in the water, reflecting light this way and that, looking like a fish in trouble. Spinners tend to be smaller and have a free-swivelling attachment like the flattened bowl of a spoon, which rotates 360 degrees around the body of the lure as it's retrieved through the water.

Plugs are slightly different. Originally made from heavily varnished wood, they now mainly come with hollow plastic bodies filled with all manner of wonders – tiny reflective surfaces that fool bigger fish into thinking they're fish scales, mini ball bearings that click and clack, propellers on the front that create yet more

vibrations to attract inquisitive predators, and jointed bodies that allow the different parts of the plug to move independently.

There are different kinds of plugs too – floating and diving, neutral buoyancy plugs which sit where they are in the water when you stop retrieving, fast and slow divers and more, usually regulated by a metal 'lip' attached to the front of the plug. They often have two sets of treble hooks – one at the tail and one in the middle, hanging down to catch fish hitting them from deeper water.

Species profile: The grayling

Extraordinarily beautiful fish, easily distinguished by its sail-like fin – and by the fact that most anglers will never catch one. They like the same environment as trout – clear, fast-flowing chalk streams – and if anything are even more sensitive to pollution, which partly goes to explain their scarcity. Soft-mouthed, fast-biting and hard-fighting, especially on light tackle. Try trotting for them.

Good for: Raising the spirits on a freezing winter's day.

Deadbaits

Dead fish – often dead sea fish like herrings, sardines, sprats and mackerel – are used by anglers after pike or eels; half a mackerel or a whole sardine are especially good because their oily scent is very attractive. Deadbaits are often used partially frozen because otherwise they tend to slide off the hook and end up in another angler's lap.

Widely available from tackle shops, you can ledger a deadbait on the bottom (predators are spectacularly lazy and often scavenge for dead fish) or wobble it back as if it were a spinner; either way is very effective.

Live baiting? People still do it but we're not in favour. Dead baiting is just as effective and while the debate over whether or not angling is harmful to fish continues to swing this way and that, we have no doubts that sticking two treble hooks into the body of a live fish is both cruel and unnecessary.

Top ingredients for groundbait

Groundbait is the stuff you lob into the spot where you're fishing in order to attract fish to your hook bait. It's a good idea to include a few samples of whatever you're fishing with but otherwise, try these ingredients.

- fine breadcrumb
- sweetcorn (don't forget the liquid in the tin)
- casters (pupating maggots)
- dead maggots (they don't wriggle into the soft bottom of the lake or river)
- hempseed
- curry powder
- vanilla essence or honey
- beer (though it seems a waste)

Use cricket ball-sized portions for feeding close in and tangerine-sized ones if you're using a catapult. Yes, there are plenty of ready-made mixes available, but making your own is more fun.

Chum

This is groundbait for predators and there are a gazillion recipes. Try this: four cups of fish-flavoured cat biscuits, four tinned hot dogs, a tablespoon of garlic powder and water to cover. Blend. Leave for an hour then blend again. Put inside two plastic bags and freeze. To use, remove from bags, drill hole through middle and secure with string, then lob out into the water. Retrieve string when you're finished.

 83

Dry and wet flies

Flies for catching trout, salmon and grayling are divided into two main types[1] – wet and dry. One is fished below the surface of the water while the other floats on top of it.

In the main, wet flies are designed to attract fish using shape and colour, rather than by imitating a specific insect, nymph or other underwater bug; there are exceptions of course, such as the Cased Caddis and the Walker's Mayfly Nymph.

Dry flies are made from material that floats, and tend to be designed in imitation of one insect or another – often a mayfly, caddis fly or olive – at various stages in their life cycle. Trout anglers will often use a miniature pump to examine the content of a fish's stomach to see what they're eating and then try and imitate it with a fly in their box.

In addition, you'll hear fly anglers refer to nymphs, bugs, hairwings, streamers and plenty of other weird and wondrous fly types.

1. 'Proper' fly anglers should look away now.

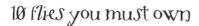

10 flies you must own

Here's a caveat. There are thousands of fly patterns and every time an angler chooses one, he spends the rest of the day thinking about the ones he didn't choose. Some anglers fish but a couple of patterns through the course of a season, thus negating the need to make a decision at all. That said:

Dry flies
- Adams (size 14–18 – also consider parachute variant)
- Deer-hair sedge (10–16)
- Shipman's buzzer (14–18 – claret and fiery brown especially)

Wet flies
- Black and peacock spider (14–18)
- Soldier palmer (10–16)
- Invicta (10–14)

Nymph
- Hare's ear (10–16, weighted and unweighted)
- Black buzzer (10–18)
- Damsel nymph (10–14)

BONUS FLY: catches fish literally everywhere
- Black woolly bugger (8–12, weighted and unweighted)

Salmon flies

Generally bigger than trout flies, salmon flies also come with single, double and treble hooks and many are what's called 'tube' flies, where the fly itself is separate from the hook. This is an extremely versatile system which allows anglers to match the fly to the size of the hook; flies like this tend to last longer, too, as the man-made fly lives on after the hook has gone rusty.

But what's really fun about salmon flies are the names. As in: Hairy Mary, Willie Gunn, Stoat's Tail, Munro Killer, Meg In Her Braws, Garry Dog, Thunder and Tosh.

Tying your own flies

The great angler and author H. T. Sheringham once wrote that if he were to start fishing all over again, he'd learn how to tie flies before learning how to cast them.[1] Many anglers would agree, and we know plenty who get almost as much satisfaction from tying a fly as they do in catching a fish with it. It takes plenty of gear – vice, sharp fine-pointed scissors,

1. Trout Fishing Memories and Morals, *pp.101–102.*

hackle pliers, bobbin holder, whip finish tool, dubbing needle, tying thread, and then loads of materials like tinsel, wool, chenille, floss, feather fibre, dubbing, Marabou, cock hackles and more. And good eyes and a steady hand.

So there you are, staring gimlet-eyed at the water. You imagine the fish beneath the surface going about their impenetrable aquatic business and then turn to the tackle that's piled neatly next to you on the bank. At which point you conclude that all you've done so far is spend money – which is easy. Now comes the hard part.

Species profile: The gudgeon

Only grows to a few ounces but is often one of the first fish young anglers catch and is captivatingly different from a roach, a bleak or a dace, thanks to its mottled colouring, barbules on either side of the mouth for feeling up the bottom and a mouth that points down, ready for action. Also has the best Latin name of any fish in this book – *Gobio gobio*.

Good for: Inspiring young anglers and keeping old anglers happy when other, pickier fish aren't biting.

Species profile: The roach

A signature fish for many anglers because it's one of the first fish they catch, the roach inhabits still and running water and grows to four pounds or so. A 1 lb (0.45 kg) fish is considered good and a two pounder (0.9 kg) the fish of a lifetime. Where other fish smell fishy, roach have a kind of piscine perfume that is almost fragrant.

Good for: Reminding you why you went fishing in the first place.

Species profile: The rudd

Like a glorious, golden roach with a protruding lower lip and a rounder shape, rudd are less common than they used to be and big ones are much harder to find. Although primarily surface feeders, they can be caught on the bottom as well.

Good for: Plenty of bites on a hot day, often even before the float has had time to settle.

CHAPTER FOUR

TECHNIQUES

Most fish prefer to hang about on the bottom of whatever pond, lake or river that you're fishing. There are plenty of exceptions – carp and rudd often prefer the surface, trout rise to take flies, pike and perch cruise at all depths – but in the main, the trick is to present the bait in a natural way and then get it down onto the bottom where the fish are waiting. This chapter looks at some of the favoured methods for doing just that.

float fishing

A float is a brightly coloured, pencil-shaped
device made of plastic – in the main – that
attaches to the line either top and bottom or
bottom only, usually in a way that allows you to
move it up and down the line when necessary.
Most floats need small weights called shot to
make them stand up in the water so that only
the tip is showing. When you get a bite the float
may bob, dip, move in a single direction at an
angle or disappear completely; sometimes if a
fish takes the bait in a certain way it will even
lift out of the water.

Still-water float fishing's pretty easy because
the float stays where you put it unless it's
windy, when the line on the surface between
you and the float may bow and eventually drag
it out of position and make the bait move
unnaturally. Float fishing on rivers is usually
called 'trotting' and involves letting the current
carry the float and bait downstream – the trick
here is releasing the line from the reel smoothly
so that the bait appears to be moving naturally
with the current.

Shotting techniques

Waggler floats are popular on still waters. They're attached at the bottom end only and often fished at distance; the bulk of the shot[1] is pinched onto the line immediately under the float to allow more accurate casting. To get the bait down quickly through small fish to the bigger ones on the bottom, divide the shot between the bottom of the float and a position about 15 inches (38 cm) from the hook. To sink the bait more slowly, bulk the shot under the float but add a couple of small ones further down the line. For trotting, try stringing out the shot evenly, leaving a 15 inch (38 cm) gap at the bottom.

Before you add any shot, you need to make sure your bait is on the bottom by attaching a weight to the hook, called a plummet. Guess the depth and cast it out into the swim. Float disappears? Make it deeper. Float lies flat on the surface? Make it shallower. Float cocks upright with just the tip showing? Just right. Remove the plummet, add the shot and you're off.

1. Shot are soft, round weights with a slit in them so they can be squeezed onto the line. They are used to 'cock' a float so that it sits upright in the water. Without shot, a typical float will lie flat on the surface.

91

Detecting a bite

This is the best bit. For every species of fish, there's a different bite. Bream are deliberate, rudd dart at a bait and then wander off with it while tench often pick a bait up off the bottom, sometimes taking the weight of the smaller shot nearer the hook and making the float 'lift' out of the water slightly as it becomes more buoyant. Perch take it with a bob-bob-bob and then carry it off to their lair, while a carp alternates between something similar and hitting the bait like a rollercoaster.

Barbel equivocate. Sometimes their bites are as shy as crucian carp, other times, you're as likely to lose the rod; chub often play the same trick. Bites also change with the seasons. Some winter bites are so delicate that they're easy to miss, as if the fish are out of the habit, unsure of what they're supposed to be doing; other times, they're clearly ravenous and give the impression that they'd climb out and eat your sandwiches as well if they could.

Unusual ways to catch fish

1. **Dogs** – In Hokkaido, Japan, fishermen send two teams of 20 dogs, 65 ft (20 m) apart into the sea; at a signal from the shore, the two lead dogs swim towards each other to form a horsehoe, then all the dogs turn to the shore, driving the fish before them.

2. **Remoras** – These suckerfish have line tied round their tails and are then released back into the sea. When they attach themselves to a larger fish, both get reeled in.

3. **Wool** – Worms are threaded onto wool and the whole thing is wrapped into a ball, attached to a rod and reel with a strong line and dropped into the water. No hook necessary, eels get their teeth caught in the wool. Salmon will also take brightly coloured bits of wool, tied to a hook and fished under a float.

4. **Rowing boats** – Jam the boat across a stream leading up from the sea to a lake. Mullet making their way to freshwater are 'tuned' to jump obstacles and so end up flapping about on the deck.

Ledgering

Ledgers are weights with some kind of eye attached to them (often via a built-in swivel) through which you thread the line. The most basic rig goes like this: Line comes from rod and goes through the eye in the ledger. Tie hook on other end. Pull on hook and the line should run freely through the eye of the ledger. Measure out the 'trail' between the ledger and the hook and pinch a shot on there. Now, when you cast and tighten the line up to the ledger, the shot will act as a stopper, yet when the fish tugs on the bait, it will allow the line to run through the ledger eye, indicating a bite.

Fish a longer trail on rivers if you want a small bait to move more naturally in the current; fish a shorter one in very weedy swims because it gives you more control.

The most popular ledger weight is still the Arlesey bomb, named after Arlesey Lake, where its inventor, Dick Walker, first used it. Flattened Arlesey bombs are good for holding the bottom in fast water, and we still use 'bullets' – round leads with a hole drilled

through the middle that roll along the bottom of the river.

You can replace the ledger with a swimfeeder – a weighted plastic tub about the size of a 35 mm film canister with holes in it. Feeders can be enclosed (use maggots here which escape through the holes) open-ended (use maggots packed in groundbait) or caged (use groundbait with particle baits like sweetcorn).

A letter rig

Replace the basic rig with this. Attach a snaplink swivel (a swivel with a clasp) to ledger or feeder so you can change between different kinds, and thread line through that. Pop a plastic bead on the line as a stopper. Tie a swivel to the end of the line. Take another piece of line and tie that to the other end of the swivel; tie hook to the other end of that. Leave an inch or two (20–50 mm) between the bead and the swivel; the hook length can be lighter line if the fish are finicky. This rig lets you change feeders and ledgers quickly and the swivel helps prevent kinking which can damage the line.

Using 'the method'

Although it may sound like it, 'the method' is not a Californian self-improvement 'philosophy' but an innovative way to use a feeder that packs the groundbait on the outside. Here's how it works.

The method feeder is open – it looks a bit like the back end of a playing dart – and has a lengthways hole through the middle. Thread the line through this. Thread on a small bead – to act as a shock absorber – and tie on a snaplink swivel. Take six inches (15 cm) of 8–12 lb line or braid for the hooklength and tie a loop in the end. Hook the clasp of the snaplink swivel through the loop.

Use method-mix groundbait (this has the right, stiff-but-sticky consistency) and pack it round the frame of the feeder. Once we've baited the hook we press that into the groundbait mix on the feeder as well. Shape the whole thing to make it aerodynamic and cast out. For best effect, try and hit the same spot each time.

Detecting ledger bites

These fall into two camps – electronic (an alarm goes off) and mechanical (something bends or moves). Battery-powered electronic bite alarms screw onto the top of rod rests and bank sticks. You rest your rod on them as normal but in between the 'v' they have a sensor which sounds an alarm and flashes a light when line is pulled through them. This allows carp anglers to go fishing and go to sleep at the same time. Just kidding.[1]

Electronic alarms have their place, especially if you're fishing a very long session over a number of days, but we prefer to keep our wits about us and only use them sparingly. They make a racket too.

These days, a mechanical alarms basically means using a quiver tip – this is an end section of the rod that's a lot lighter and bendier than the main thing – it's usually brightly coloured too. Sit with the rod at an angle to the water, tighten up to the bait and when the fish takes, the rod tip knocks or pulls round.

1. No, we're not.

freelining

One of the most exciting forms of fishing uses no tackle at all apart from the line, the hook and the bait. It's called freelining. Fly-fishing types do it all the time and understand the beauty and the purity of having as little between you and the fish as possible. We've seen some people reeling in rigs so heavy and complicated that they can hardly tell if they got a fish on the line or not. Freelining's the opposite.

Bigger baits work best for freelining because you need some weight to cast. We like to fish one or two dog biscuits floating on the surface for carp, or send a large piece of luncheon meat trundling down the river bed for barbel, or drop a lump of cheese paste into a likely looking chub hole. Not having a float or the weight of end tackle does make the bait harder to control but it's a very sensitive way of fishing and the results are excellent.

> ❛ It is not so much different kinds
> of fish which require different methods as
> different kinds of water. ❜
>
> *Coarse Fishing*, H. D. Turing

Lure fishing

Fish that like to eat other fish (and we mean really like it as opposed to fish like barbel that will occasionally snaffle a minnow or something) are lazy and spend most of their time moseying around on the lookout for smaller fish that are in trouble. So, the purpose of a lure is to mimic the same.

Lures don't have to be that realistic to fool a fish but they do need to be attached to the mainline using a wire trace; that's because a pike's toothy grin isn't just for show and it'll make short work of monofilament or braid.

Species profile: The gwyniad

Commonly found in lakes and rivers and the only known fish that can read anglers' minds, thus allowing it to elude them time and time again. Has also been known to steal anglers' cars from the car park just because it can.[1]

Good for: A tall tale or two (as if you hadn't guessed).

1. Since the Gwyniad is only found in one lake – Llyn Tegid in Bala, Wales – we can say pretty much what we like since most of you will never get near one.

The retrieve and the take

Lure fishing involves casting out the spinner or plug and then reeling it in. You can do this mechanically at a steady turning pace but most anglers believe that if you vary the speed at which you retrieve the lure, then it will mimic the fluttering actions of a sick or dying fish more accurately. Some lures are designed to rise and fall through the water depending on the rate of retrieve – so it's worth practising in clear shallow water so you can watch how the lure behaves.

When you're casting a lure, don't just cast straight out – we work in a clockwise semi-circle starting from the margins on our left and working round to the ones on our right.

Anglers bedevilled by uncertainty over what is and what isn't a bite can relax. When a pike or other predator hits a lure… you'll know about it alright.

How to cast a fly

In general fishing, casting is pretty easy because you've got something on the end of the line (a ledger, a float and weights, a lure and so on) to work with. Fly-fishing is different because the business end (where the fly is) is actually lighter than the main fly line – therefore you must use the weight of the mainline itself to propel the fly where you want it to go. This involves a curious, rhythmic back and forth with the rod which is known as the overhead cast.

Watching a proper fly-fisherman is a joy. They can put a fly on a trout's nose at thirty paces; they can avoid the trees behind them by using the roll cast, or guide fly and line round an obstacle in the river such as a rock, with a gentle turn of the wrist partway through the cast.

Although purists will tell you otherwise, it doesn't matter too much if your technique is less than perfect. The main thing to avoid is turning the rod into a whip and thrashing the water with your line – this will scare the fish off.

101

Casting a fly properly is one of the great skills of angling, but the bones of it are simple enough. Imagine you're standing in front of the face of a clock. Start with the rod pointed at 8.00 o'clock. Bring the rod up smartly to midday and allow the line to extend behind you. When you feel the line pulling the tip of the rod into the 1.00 or 2.00 o'clock position, bring the rod forwards smoothly through the arc to 8.00 o'clock again.

Start with about 10–20 feet (3–6 m) of line out in front of you and then, as you find a rhythm and are able to extend the line in front of you fully each time, pull a bit more of the reel with the other hand – let this go as you bring the rod forward again and it'll shoot out through the rings.

Go off and practise for 30 years and you'll soon get the hang of it.

When to strike

If we knew the answer to that, then we'd have caught many more fish than we actually have. The obvious ones? When the float goes under and stays there, when the rod tip bends round as if someone's tugging your sleeve rather than trying to pick your pocket, when the pike hits the lure, when the line runs from the reel, when the line that waves across the surface suddenly pulls straight. The less obvious? When the rod tip bent against the current suddenly drops back, when the float lifts, when there's a pluck on the line or rod tip so gentle it barely registers (sometimes a big fish, this one), when the float moves downstream faster than the current and when it moves more slowly.

Watch for false bites too – fish physically knocking into the line or the float, river debris in autumn rubbing against the line and summer weeds waving into the line.

'But bite the perch will, and that very boldly. And, as one has wittily observed, if there be twenty or forty in a hole, they may be, at one standing, all catched one after another; they being, as he says, like the wicked of the world, not afraid, though their fellows and companions perish in their sight.'

The Compleat Angler, Sir Izaak Walton

Wet and dry fly fishing

Since fly fishing is normally such a complicated business, it's refreshing to discover that wet and dry fly fishing is exactly what it sounds like. Dry flies float on the surface of a lake or river and – usually – imitate a specific kind of insect. Wet flies are designed to sink and then be retrieved by the angler so as to mimic aquatic insects in a more general sense either struggling to the surface or sinking in despair. Wet-fly fishermen cunningly often use two or three flies arranged on the end of the line to increase their chances.

Species profile: The ide

Small silver fish that looks a bit like a skinny roach or maybe a dace, minus the flatter, more interesting head. Although found in still waters they spawn in rivers, so need access to running water. In larger fish, the fins take on an attractive pink hue.

Good for: Pretending you've caught one when it's actually a little roach.

Playing, landing and unhooking

Small fish are easy. You should be able to swing in anything smaller than six inches (15 cm), grab it with your free hand and then unhook it carefully. If you need to hold the fish for longer than a few seconds, use a wet cloth. Make sure you have and know how to use a disgorger, either the forceps kind for larger hooks or for when it's just inside the mouth, or the pencil kind which slides down the line and over the shaft when a fish is deeply hooked.

Take your time with larger fish – a bullied fish will still have bags of energy and flop about all over the bank damaging itself. Trust your tackle and adjust the drag of a fixed-spool reel to give line when it needs to; use the ratchet on a centrepin to do the same. Keep the rod up and let it do the work for you.

When the fish is ready to come in, sink the landing net in the water and draw the fish over it, rather than trying to bring the net towards it. For larger fish, use a padded unhooking mat to protect them.

Pike are a special case. For such ferocious fish they fare badly unless well-treated. Try and go with someone more experienced for a few trips to get the hang of handling them. Pike should be turned upside down for unhooking and you'll need a strong glove and long-nosed forceps.

All unhooking is made easier thanks to barbless hooks and by keeping the use of treble hooks to a minimum.

Species profile: The perch

With their striped sides and spiny dorsal fin, perch are the most distinctive of coarse fish. Small ones are eager to take any bait (and quick to swallow it – you have been warned) while the giants grow big by eating their smaller cousins. Perch numbers ebb and flow more than most other fish but luckily, they're making something of a comeback.

Good for: A sore hand if you don't hold them properly.

Caring for fish

Don't keep a fish out of the water for longer than you have to. Want to take a photo? Make sure your camera is to hand and you know how to use it. We photograph fish while they're still in the landing net with the rod, reel and float positioned above them for scale. If you've got a friend with you, they can take the picture.[1] Weigh fish in a proper sack or still in the landing net, then subtract the weight of the net.

Having carefully unhooked that three-ounce roach, don't just toss it back into the water; take it to the swim next door, hold it under the water and let it swim off. This is especially important with fish like barbel and pike which tend to exhaust themselves during the fight – hold their heads facing upstream in running water and wait for them to move off before letting go.

OK, it's going to get more difficult from now on. You've got some gear, you understand a bit about how to use it, but now you've got you've got to discover what kind of angler you want to be. The pages that follow may help. Then again…

1. Remember to hold the fish slightly in front of you so it looks bigger.

Duffer's fortnight

It's 2 June 1973. The river is alive with mayflies hatching and the trout are going bonkers. Hands shaking, he ties on something resembling a mayfly, fumbles a cast and watches in wonder as a two-pounder rises from the depths and sips at the fly. He strikes, his face lit by a stupid grin. The little fly rod hoops over against the evening sky. In the distance, the train between Newbury and Hungerford slows as millions of tiny insects take to the air. No more, no more.

Where to fish

Interestingly enough – or we hope interestingly enough – the spot where you choose to fish is called something different depending on the style of fishing you're engaged in. Coarse anglers call this a *swim*,[1] while game fishermen refer to it as a *beat*. Sea anglers call it a *mark*.

---

1. *Perhaps because they fall in more often?*

CHAPTER FIVE

TRADITION OR TECHNOLOGY?

hile you can of course be any kind of angler you want to be, there's a distinction to be drawn between fish counters and fishermen. Fish counters measure success purely in the number and size of the fish they catch; fishermen are usually fishing for something other than fish – though they enjoy catching them well enough should they come along.

At the risk of coming over all misty-eyed about the good old days we're going to spend this chapter examining these two schools of fishing

through the prism of tackle and techniques. While not perfect, we've decided to label the pair 'tradition' and 'technology' in order to see if one is a 'better' way to fish than the other. This should end well, then…

Philosophy versus purpose

There's a tendency among anglers of a certain age to hark back to the past when fish were more plentiful, rivers ran cleaner, lakes brimmed with trout, you could catch rudd in the local pond and carp had yet to be domesticated.[1] In fact, if you come across any early photographs of anglers with their catch you'll see that fishing back then was more like wholesale slaughter; fish were poorly treated, not returned, big ones were stuffed and others kept all day in badly designed, overcrowded keepnets. Pike were routinely landed using a gaff – basically a giant hook on the end of a pole which was hooked into the soft skin between their lower jaws – big, beautiful roach were hooked live with two treble hooks and despatched beneath a pike bung to die slowly…[2] So maybe the past isn't necessarily all it's cracked up to be.

1. *What else do you call something that you feed every day and has a name?*
2. *Still happens. Shouldn't. Fish with a deadbait instead.*

Modern anglers tend to have fishes' best interests at heart. It's partly self-interest because healthy waters and fish stocks mean better angling, and partly because it takes a heart of stone not to find a three-pound crucian carp a wondrous thing. Somewhere along the line, however, it's gone a bit wrong. Much of modern fishing is all about 'bagging up', catching fish after fish after fish, all day, every day. Commercial fisheries are created and stocked with fast-growing, hard-eating carp to fulfil this desire, close seasons when fish and bank and angler could take a break are abandoned, baits are brewed up that make fish eat, even when they're not hungry.

As you'll see in the pages that follow, we're not against technology per se, but we disagree fundamentally with those who say that the enjoyment you get from fishing can be measured and weighed at the end of the day like a keepnet full of bent and battered fish.

All together now – there's more to fishing than catching fish.

III

Cane vs. carbon fibre

Most anglers don't own a cane rod and that's almost entirely down to cost. They don't see the point in spending several hundred pounds on something when they could get a modern alternative for a fraction of the price.

Fact is, coarse cane rods are usually hand-built and based on one or two famous rod types – typically the Mark IV Avon or the Mark IV Carp rod[1] – and expense aside, these patterns don't always suit the modern angler. At the same time, a good carbon rod will also last a lifetime, generally accepts wear and tear a bit better and is more suited to being chucked in the back of the car.

In use, a cane rod is livelier than a carbon one and some people find them, er... less predictable when casting a large bait. But you'll soon get used to it. For fly fishing, carbon absolutely gets the job done but cane fly-fishing rods are things of joy, full stop.

---

1. *designed by Richard Walker (see pages 172 and 174).*

'Note also, that many used to fish for a Salmon with a ring of wire on the top of their rod, through which the line may run to as great a length as is needful, when he is hooked. And to that end, some use a wheel about the middle of their rod, or near their hand, which is to be observed better by seeing one of them than by a large demonstration of words.'

The Compleat Angler, Sir Izaak Walton

The action of a rod

The bend of the rod is called the 'action' and there are basically two kinds – all through and tip. As the name suggests, all-through action rods bend from the tip pretty much all the way through to the butt – these give you a great 'feel' for a hooked fish and help you cast further. Tip-action rods are better for striking but less good for casting. In fly fishing it's the other way round – tip-action rods are better at long casts and for landing bigger fish, through-action rods are better for short casts where accuracy is important.

Centrepin vs. fixed-spool reel

Most people use fixed-spool reels. They're geared so that one turn of the handle equates to multiple turns of the spool, which means you can retrieve line more quickly. They can cast further because the weight of the end tackle pulls line from the static spool over the lip, and a properly filled spool offers little or no resistance – the rod and reel act a bit like one of those throwing sticks that dogs (and dog owners) love.

The bird's nest

Sometimes the physics of fishing overwhelms both the line and the reel and in seconds you can find yourself confronted with a terrible tangle of line that's just appeared from nowhere. It's tempting to try and untangle this, but don't bother. The line will be weakened and you won't be able to rely on it.

Although the whole point of a fixed-spool reel is that the spool doesn't rotate, you can adjust it so that it will rotate when a fish pulls hard enough. This allows you to concentrate on trying to control a fighting fish rather than worrying about the line snapping.

A centrepin is a different beast entirely. One turn of the reel equals one turn of the spool. Casting? You'll need to strip line from the reel first with one hand and then use the other to hold the rod and cast the tackle out, making it much harder – though not impossible – to cast very far with a centrepin. However, it can't be beat, for trotting in a fast river where the strength of the current is enough to set the reel spinning and pull line off.

Centrepin reels usually have a ratchet which stops them from rotating freely; this is extremely useful when playing a larger fish because – like the drag on a fixed-spool reel – it lets the fish take line grudgingly so you don't have to worry about putting too much strain on it.

Natural baits vs. the boilie

A tricky one, this. Artificial, shop-bought baits are so damned attractive to fish – halibut-flavoured pellets sweetened with strawberry essence… come on, even we want to give it a go – that it's tempting to give in and bag up. And yet, and yet.

We believe there's something intrinsically wrong in a bait that is beyond attractive and instead can chemically seduce a fish into gobbling it down, even if the fish isn't really hungry. It's the enhancers and appetite stimulators of these Frankenfoods that we think tip the likely result too far in the angler's favour.

So, should it be all bread flake and maggots, sweetcorn, worms and bread past, or is it OK to use something that has ingredients like pre-digested fish and crustacean meals, caseins, lactalbumin, calf milk replacer, bird foods, squid and fish enhancers? In the end, every angler decides for themselves, and despite our leanings towards old-fashioned baits, we're not beyond blagging a bit of trout paste or the odd strawberry pellet when things are going slowly.

How's about this? Fishing should be like a seduction. You should be able to choose the right venue, pick the time to meet, present your wares at their most attractive, maybe even spray on a bit of perfume – but you shouldn't be allowed to cover yourself in pheronomes, sit in a bar in your vest and pajama bottoms eating a bag of cheese and onion crisps while passing members of the opposite sex – unable to resist – throw themselves at you.

Species profile: The pike

Nature at her finest, the pike is built like no other coarse fish. Huge mouth, teeth that slope slightly backwards, long, lean body and most of its fins gathered at the back from where they give the pike its legendary Lamborghini-style acceleration. So camouflaged that anglers can walk right past one hanging in the margins, a foot from the bank, close enough to touch.

Good for: Scaring the hell out of dozy anglers.

Comparing rigs

Let's look at how technology and tradition impact the way we set up our end tackle.

For years we fished like this for carp. Ten-pound breaking-strain mainline threaded through an Arlesey bomb ledger so it hangs about 12 inches (30 cm) out the other side. Pinch on a shot to stop the bomb sliding off the line. Tie on a size 4 hook with a four-and-a-half-turn blood knot; finish with a lump of luncheon meat the size of a 35 mm film container. Cast out. The bait sinks into the muddy debris of the lake floor and the oils from the luncheon meat seep out into the water, hopefully ready to attract a passing carp. We wait.

Then we started fishing like this: Ten-pound breaking-strain mainline threaded through a bit of rubber tube, threaded through a safety clip, another bit of rubber tube and tied onto a link swivel. An Arlesey bomb is attached to a separate link swivel which is in turn attached to the safety clip. We then take a 9-inch (23 cm) braid hook length, thread it through the eye of

a size 4 hook and pull until about an inch (25 mm) of line extends from the bend of the hook. Tie a knotless knot in that end then take the other end of the braid, wrap it round the hook a few times and then pull it back through the hook eye. Tie a swivel onto this end and then hook that over the end of the link swivel on the mainline. Thread the bait – a pop-up boilie – over the bit of line extending past the hook where the knotless knot is so only a tiny bit of the loop shows through and then push in a little shop-bought stopper (or a bit of matchstick) to secure it. Just to be clear – the hook and the bait are linked by the line but entirely separate. Finally, add a shot about 4 inches (100 mm) from the hook. Why? Because we're using a pop-up boilie which floats above the debris on the bottom of the lake so the fish can find it. Sneaky, huh? Now we wait. But probably not for quite as long.

Bite detection

For the modern angler there's only one way to detect a bite from a big carp or pike or catfish or even tench – and that's to use an electronic bite alarm. Such devices look like plump rod-rest tops and inside are powered by batteries that give visual and audio alarms when you get a bite (early versions were called 'optonics').

Many anglers in for a long session will have several rods each with its own bite alarm which sounds when the sensors detect the line being pulled off by a fish. Alarms typically have several controls – volume (important when it's windy), tone (so you can tell which rod has got the bite) and one or more lights (again so you can tell which rod has got the bite at night); some have an extra light which comes on after the 'bite light' is extinguished. This is technology at its most cunning. Think about it. It's night and you get a bite but instead of developing, the fish drops the bait and moseys off – you need to know which rod to reel in and re-bait; hence the second light.

All these flashing lights and buzzers can make a carp lake a noisy place. Add the regular 'fpishh' of beer cans being opened and it can feel more like sitting next to a fruit machine in the pub. Smells the same, too.

Of course, if you come a little way round the lake to this quiet corner you'll find an entirely different scene. Here an angler has cast out and as darkness falls he's pulled a large loop of line from between the reel and first rod ring and now holds it between his fingers; if he gets a bite he'll feel the tug and by the time the line's been pulled free he'll be ready to strike. In silence.

Next door is another angler who's fixed a ball of paste to his line between the reel and first ring. The weight of the paste pulls the line tight and if it should twitch and then rise until the line is taut, the angler will know he's got a bite.

Next to him is a third angler who's reeled in and gone to sleep.

Supplementary gear

We've always thought it suspect that an angler would need a wheelbarrow (or a snazzier, more expensive, somehow 'angling' version of the same) in order to get their gear from the car park to the waterside. But when you see what some fishermen consider essential (yes, you can buy a collapsible kitchen sink) it's no wonder that they look – and occasionally sound – like mules, winding up a mountainside. Bed chair, bivvy tent, sleeping bag, three rods and reels, rod pods, landing net, unhooking mat, weigh sling, wet sack, three tons of bait, kettle, stove, gas light, plates, cutlery – there are people living off the grid in the Utah hills who are less prepared than this lot.

By contrast, we're big fans of travelling light. One rod (very occasionally two but never fished at the same time), an inflatable pillow for a seat, small bag/wicker creel, mini, extendable rod rests, poncho, some sweetcorn, bit of bread, half a tin of luncheon meat. You can catch nearly anything with that.

Dick Walker catches Clarissa[1]

In an interview, Richard Walker describes breaking the carp record on 13 September 1952 at Redmire Pool.

'We got a rough weight because we hadn't got a spring balance that read high enough, so we tied two spring balances together side by side and hung the carp in a wet sack on that, added the two readings together and got a figure of 41½ lb. Which was obviously not very accurate but it was accurate enough to let us know that we'd beaten the former record which was 31¼ lb by a fairly comfortable margin. So we put the fish back in the wet sack, tied up the mouth and put it back in the water so it wouldn't take any harm, and fairly early the next morning I got to a phone and rang London Zoo and said "Do you want a 40 lb carp?" And they said "We've got a 14 lb carp." And I said "No, forTY, not fourTEEN." It was very accurately weighed the next morning with an inspector of weights and measures and one or two witnesses present and found to weigh 44 lb, and it resided in the zoo for many, many years after that.'

1. Or as he apparently preferred to call it, Ravioli.

A good read

Pick up an angling magazine these days and it feels like you're being shouted at. Exclamation marks abound! You'll be exhorted to catch more! And catch faster! You'll be told that you're bonkers about bream! Or crazy about carp!

Behind the scenes of course there's the subtler (but not that subtle) sub-text that's telling you to buy the latest rod or reel or line or hook, seat or brolly, lure or bivvy slippers (actually you probably won't catch any carp unless you buy these new 'stealth' bivvy slippers), camouflaged, fingerless gloves (as used by snipers in Desert Storm) and a personal jetpack[1] so you can hover above the lake, spotting the biggest fish from above.

This tabloid tone has turned modern angling publishing into a wasteland of tips and tricks and techniques – almost all of which require you to buy something or other in order to follow them; celebrity anglers abound, as do

1. Note – at the time of writing, jetpacks are not real.

sponsorships, tackle deals and endorsements, monogrammed clothing and pointless, repetitive DVDs.

Now we're not necessarily advocating a return to plus-fours, bicycles, cane rods, creels and deerstalkers or the literature that went with them, but we do feel there's a place for books and magazines that remember why we go fishing in the first place, that examine the space it occupies in our lives above and beyond the mechanics of catching. For years we've felt like a voice in the wilderness as everything around us became more commercialised, more dedicated to the great god of catching more and catching faster.

And yet. We hear that one magazine has changed its format, hiving off the tips into a separate section, leaving the main magazine with a bit more space to breathe, and to be – dare we hope? – a bit more reflective. Maybe it'll even find time to talk about some of the challenges that face fishing in the 21st century – or maybe it'll just dial the volume down a bit.

The close season vs.
open all hours

Originally introduced at the end of the 19th century to protect fisheries from the impact of angling when it was thought that coarse fish spawned in spring and when few fish were returned to the water alive, the close season runs from 15 March to 15 June inclusive. Since 1994, it still takes effect on rivers, streams and drains but not on still waters, where it is down to the discretion of the riparian owner. The result? Many waters are fished 24 hours a day, 365 days a year.

This is being driven by economics – pure and simple – and by fishery owners taking advantage of the modern angler's sense of entitlement and impatience. I can get a hamburger at three in the morning or find a bar that's still open, or watch an on-demand movie whenever I like, so why shouldn't I be able to go fishing when it suits me and my busy schedule?

Here's why...

Because waiting is good for the soul. If you wait until you can actually afford something before you buy it, you'll appreciate it more; and if you've got to wait three months, watching as spring turns to summer, then when you return to the waterside you'll be refreshed and reinvigorated and you'll – maybe – feel a little like you did when you were a kid.

There are other benefits too. The spawning argument may have been debunked, but there's no doubt that rivers and lakes need a chance to recover, and banks, paths, gates and stiles need the same – and anglers need a break too, even if they don't necessarily want one.

So don't be an open-all-hours fisherman. Instead, consider observing your own close season, even if it's only for a month. Do something else. Spend more time at home. Read some books, sort your tackle out. Think about fishing. Remember – good for the soul.

Right, having encouraged you to take a break from fishing, we're now going to whet your appetite again by looking at some of the signature fish you can catch from different countries around the world. Bags packed and passports at the ready? Hang on to your hat…

 127

Recipe: Baked pike

You will need: one or two pike, stuffing, one egg,
breadcrumbs, ¼ lb (0.11 kg) of butter.

Preparation: Scale fish, remove gills, wash and
wipe well; stuff and then sew up. Fix the tail in
the mouth with a skewer, brush with egg and
sprinkle breadcrumbs over entire body, then
baste with the butter. Pop in a well-heated oven
for one hour. Serve him with roasted potatoes
and greens.

Species profile: The zander

Not, as originally thought, a cross between a
pike and a perch (they even used to be called
pike-perch) but a relative of the American
walleye, the zander isn't native to the UK and
occasionally appears on lists of imported
'pests'.[1] They have big mad eel-eyes and thrive
in slow, murky water.

Good for: A real surprise since they're still not
that common.

1. *Though not on ours – see page 19.*

CHAPTER SIX

ANGLING ADVENTURES

Although you can have an angling adventure in the stream at the bottom of your garden or the pond at the end of the lane, increasing numbers of fishermen are setting their sights further afield. In this chapter we're going to take a whistle stop tour round some of the finest fishing the planet has to offer. Get it while it's still going…

A world of fishing

1. British Columbia, Canada – Sturgeon
2. Eleuthera, the Bahamas – Bonefish
3. Rio Grande, Tierra Del Fuego, Argentina – Sea trout
4. Tyrifjorden, Norway – Pike

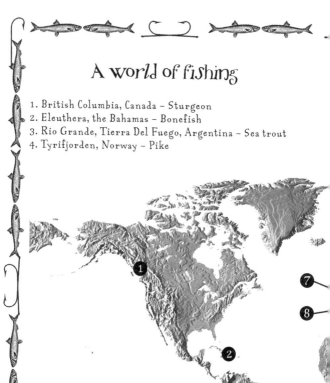

NORTH

WEST   EAST

SOUTH

5. Kola Peninsula, Russia – Atlantic salmon
6. Lake Nasser, Egypt – Nile perch
7. Massignac, France – Carp
8. River Ebro, Spain – Catfish
9. River Cauvery, India – Mahseer
10. Province of Khovsgol, Mongolia – Taimen
11. Mataura river, New Zealand – Brown Trout

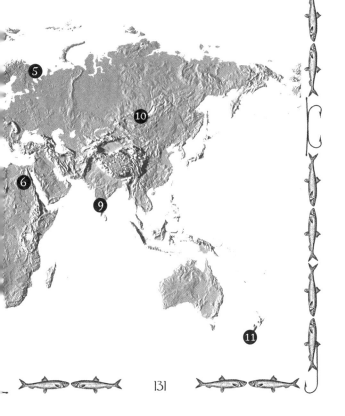

Canada: The Sturgeon
Try: The Fraser river, British Columbia

This remarkable scaleless fish, with its long snout and elongated body which looks as though it's been carved from stone, can grow to 18 feet (5.4 m) in length – though the ones typically caught in Canadian waters usually 'only' grow to between 2 and 6 feet (0.6–1.8 m). The main sturgeon season is between April and the end of November but fish can be caught all year round. Most companies can provide tackle (unless you've got some 150 lb (68 kg) breaking-strain braided line knocking about) and trips are highly organised and usually successful. The river itself is stunning and there aren't many places you can catch a freshwater fish that needs four people to hold it.

What to see: Pacific Rim National Park, home to one of the world's most unusual temperate rainforests. That's right, in Canada.

What to eat: Poutine – French fries smothered with curds of fresh cheese, topped with brown gravy.

Recipe: Roast sturgeon

You will need: veal stuffing, buttered paper, tail end of a sturgeon.

Preparations: Clean thoroughly, then bone and skin the tail before stuffing the part of the tail where the bones came from. Roll in buttered paper, tie with string and roast in a Dutch oven over a hot fire. Serve with melted butter. Takes about one hour.[1]

The piranha myth

These apparently ferocious flesh-stripping fiends are in fact relatively timid. They shoal for protection from other predators and demonstrate a keen social order by placing the larger, fertile fish in the middle of the shoal and the useless teenagers at the edge. They have a great sense of smell but rotten eyesight.

And stripping the flesh from a cow in seconds? Blame Theodore Roosevelt who supposedly brought the story back from Brazil, having seen captive fish brought to the edge of starvation, feeding on a small cow in a spectacle designed to titillate tourists.

1. Don't try this, really.

133

The Bahamas: The bonefish
Try: The Island of Eleuthera

The bonefish, all angles and big head, has a reputation as a fierce fighter, especially on fly tackle. A sea fish – often called the grey ghost – it drifts into shallow waters with the tide to feed over mudflats and, fortunately for anglers, lives in some of the world's most beautiful places. A good fish is anything that takes two hands to hold, but even the tiddlers fight like fury.

Bonefish are usually caught on the fly and because of the prevailing conditions (flat, often windy) you'll need to be relatively proficient at casting – certainly a complete beginner will find it frustrating. Note that standard freshwater fly tackle isn't suitable for saltwater fishing so you'll either need to buy or hire.

What to see: The Levy Plant Reserve; tiny 25-acre (10-hectare) national park with some of the prettiest walks in the Bahamas – visit the Tower and although only 20 feet (6 m) off the ground you'll be able to see the entire island.

What to eat: Crack conch with peas and rice (the conch is a kind of giant snail and can be chewy – ask the chef to pummel it with a wooden mallet).

Argentina: The sea trout
Try: The Rio Grande in Tierra Del Fuego

There are many magical things about the 'land of fire' at the bottom of the world, but the sea trout, which grow huge – one in four is said to weigh more than 15 lbs (6.8 kg) – are a wonder. Wading on fine gravel, even a fly-fishing novice will do well here, and the season runs from October to April with the best time being after the turn of the year, between January and March.

What to see: The Estancia Maria Behety, the largest sheep-shearing shed in the world.

What to eat: Parilla – a bowel-wincing mixed grill of steak, sausage and organ meat such as liver and kidney.

135

Norway: The pike
Try: Tyrifjorden

It's hard to get your head around the scale of Norway's lakes. Tyrifjorden is 'only' the fifth largest and it still occupies 137 square kilometres (52 square miles) and is nearly 300 metres (nearly 1,000 ft) deep in places. That's plenty of room for even a monster pike to hang out, and some of the ones here are just that – enormous, beautifully marked, never-been-caught pike – who'll fall to all the usual tactics, but especially trolling.[1]

What to see: The Spikersuppa skating rink in the middle of Oslo, one of Europe's most impressive cities.

What to eat: Farikal, a casserole of seasonal lamb and cabbage served with boiled new potatoes, cowberry sauce and crisp flatbread.

---

1. *Trolling is a method of fishing from a boat – the bait is cast into the water, the rod is made secure on the boat and the boat then moves through the water, pulling the bait behind it. It's common to fish with more than one rod when trolling.*

Russia: The Atlantic salmon
Try: The Kola Peninsula

Those who've fished them speak of the Kharlovka, Litza and Rynda rivers with something approaching awe. Wide deeps, tumbling narrows, gorges and waterfalls, these and other rivers are home to some of the finest runs of Atlantic salmon. Late May and early June are chancy but plan your trip so it takes in mid-June and early July when the rising air and water temperatures encourage the salmon to run and there are fish everywhere – typically 10 lb (4.5 kg) or bigger. You can fish on into September when there's the possibility of an enormous Osenka salmon which can weigh up to 30% more than a typical Atlantic salmon.

What to see: Pay your respects to the 118 sailors who died aboard the nuclear submarine *Kursk* by visiting the deck cabin memorial in Murmansk harbour.

What to eat: Pelmeny – unleavened dough wrapped around ground beef and onion and then boiled to make dumplings.

137

Egypt: The Nile perch
Try: Lake Nasser

Imagine a cross between a perch, a large-mouthed bass and an angry sockeye salmon in its freshwater stage, when it's got that hump thing going on; then imagine that the result also weighs 200 lb (91 kg) and you'll have some idea of what awaits in Lake Nasser. The water itself, created when the Aswan dam was built, is vast (around five and a half thousand square kilometres – over 2,100 square miles – that spans Egypt and Sudan) so companies run boats with sonar to find the fish and generally supply the tackle. Visitors can fish from dawn till dusk and obsessive anglers can also continue from the shore at night and catch large catfish who come in to scrounge scraps in the shallows.

Where to go: The great temple at Abu Simbel – built by Rameses II and dedicated to the gods Amun, Ptah and Ra-Horakhty. Almost as impressive as the perch.

What to eat: Ful medames – fava beans cooked and mashed and served with olive oil, onion, garlic, chopped parsley and a dash of lemon juice.

The fish hall of shame

Ugliest – the catfish; a cross between a skinned actual cat that's lost its bones and a used condom.

Scariest – the lizard fish; has teeth on its tongue. 'Nuff said.

Sneakiest – the angler fish; has evolved a detached spine from its dorsal fin which leans forward and waggles enticingly over an enormous tooth-infested mouth that attracts smaller fish towards their gobby grave.

Laziest – the blob fish; lives in deep water off the Australian coast, and can't even be bothered to swim. Mostly gelatinous, it just floats above the ocean floor with its mouth open.

Most disgusting – the hagfish; even a small specimen is capable of producing buckets and buckets of glutinous, sticky slime when agitated.

france: The carp
Try: Carp France in Massignac

Hugely popular with British anglers, this is high luxury fishing, the nearest thing to watching an angling programme on the telly from the comfort of your sofa. Some venues deliver bait to the swim, others breakfast; many of the big ones are more like holiday camps, with chalets, a bar, satellite TV and more. It's a wonder anyone has time to do any fishing. When they do, they're likely to catch very large carp – the average weight is usually in the high 20s, the really big fish up to 60 lbs (27.2 kg) or more.

The French countryside resonates with English anglers because it's less developed and more open – it reminds you of what the countryside was like when you were a kid. Carp feed all year round.

What to see: Explore the beautiful Charente National Forest.

What to eat: Cassoulet, slow-cooked stew with sausage or duck, goose or pork and white haricot beans, topped with cubes of fried bread.

Spain: The catfish
Try: The River Ebro

Supposedly introduced only 30 years ago by a German scientist, the catfish has thrived in the River Ebro and now provides great sport for visiting anglers and a good living for the companies that run fishing holidays. Cats are love-them-or-hate-them fish, big, ugly brutes or powerful, noble predators that fight like enormous muscular sausages – with 100 lb (45 kg) fish not untypical, you'll probably be too busy huffing and puffing yours to the bank to worry which it is. Be prepared to livebait though.

What to see: Have a complete break and go to the amazing Parc Güell in Barcelona.

What to eat: Cocido, slow-cooked stew with chicken or sausage, vegetables and chickpeas (garbanzos).

India: The mahseer
Try: The River Cauvery

The mahseer looks like a common carp that's been irradiated by an alien machine designed to give it sharper angles and edges, turn the scales to armour plate and generally make it angry enough to swim against the current in a raging river at 20 knots, while you're hanging on the other end. Mahseer can be caught on lures, with bait (crabs are best) or on flies. They can grow to 100 lb (45 kg) in weight.

Many mahseer are caught on ragi paste, an exotic variation of bread paste – millet flour mixed with water and flavoured with cumin or sometimes yeast. Turn it into cricket-ball-sized balls and boil until firm. Good luck.

What to see: Elephant and bison at the Rajiv Gandhi National Park (known locally as the Nagarhole National Park).

What to eat: Masala dosa, a crispy lentil and rice pancake filled with onion, potato and red chilli chutney.

Mongolia: The taimen
Try: The northern province of Khovsgol

Popularly dubbed 'giant, prehistoric trout', taimen are the largest, most aggressive member of the salmon family, growing to weights of 60 lb (26 kg) or more but spending their whole lives in fresh water.

Although the season starts in mid-June, the best fishing – and most comfortable conditions – are usually to be had in September. Some anglers stay in tents, while in more permanent camps there are comfortable yurts (the Mongolians call these *gers*) heated by wood stoves. Taimen fishing is always catch and release and you should fish with single, barbless hooks. Oh, and expect lots of walking or be happy to ride a small horse.

What to see: Everything. Mongolia is astonishing and unspoiled.

What to eat: Buuz, a dumpling filled with minced mutton or beef and seasoned with onion and garlic and fennel seeds.

 143

New Zealand: Brown trout
Try: The Mataura river

Since becoming home to brown trout in the 1860s, New Zealand is now a well-trodden path for anglers seeking first-class fly fishing. Although it's still possible to get off the beaten track, most anglers will fish venues like the Mataura river which winds through some of the loveliest countryside on South Island; despite being on nearly every angler's itinerary, this is still a must-visit for dry-fly fishing. Trout grow to 33 lb (15 kg) and less experienced anglers can travel with a guide who'll put them on top of fish, thus improving your chances of a big one.

What to see: It's *Lord Of The Rings* country so visit the Misty Mountains (otherwise known as the South Alps).

What to eat: Lamb pie with flaky pastry, mashed potatoes and peas.[1]

'Nay, the Royal Society have found and published lately, that there be thirty and three different kind of spiders; and yet all, for aught I know, go under that one general name of spider. And it is so with many kinds of fish, and of Trouts especially; which differ in their bigness, and shape, and spots, and colour.'

The Compleat Angler, Sir Izaak Walton

The more you fish, the more anglers you meet. And the more anglers you meet – whether in this country or overseas – the more you'll come to realise that there are certain angling archetypes that cross borders and countries and even generations. Want to know more? Turn the page. You may even recognise yourself.

five great fishy films

1. **The Host (2006)** Innocent cyprinid[1] turns into giant, be-tentacled, catfish-style monster after over-dosing on dumped formaldehyde. Eats some people, saves others for later in a pit.

2. **Frankenfish (2004)** The poster says it all – 'Welcome to the bottom of the food chain.'

3. **Sharktopus (2010)** OK, so neither are strictly fish but come on, the military have created a shark-octopus mutant and it's getting away!

4. **Piranha (2010)** That screaming sound doesn't come from the victims of the eponymous razor-toothed aqua-fiends, but rather from Oscar winners Richard Dreyfuss and Elisabeth Shue as they realise their careers are, well… you know the rest.

5. **Dinoshark (2010)** A baby dinoshark (there's little or no attempt to explain how this happened) thaws out in the Arctic and feasts on all the climate-change deniers. The look on their faces…

1. We're guessing at its carpish origins because it isn't real.

CHAPTER SEVEN

ANGLING ARCHETYPES

N ow, we all know that we're individuals and that we don't fit any stereotypes, but other people? Well that's a different kettle of you-know-what. And angling's just the same. Come with us on a journey around the banks of a typical lake and let's listen in to what they're thinking.

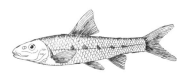

The pleasure angler

'I'll be with you in a second, I've just got to sort myself out a bit. I just threw a few bits in the back of the car and it looks like I've come out without a couple of things. Wait a minute, what's this? Hmm. OK, so I've got a spool of what looks like 50 yards of 20 lb line, a salmon spinner, a couple of pole floats, a hook tyer, a baiting needle, a bubble float half-full of – good grief, what is that?!? – and a landing-net handle. Oh and a tin of sweet corn and some dog biscuits. What I don't have is a landing net, a reel to put the spool on, a tin opener, hooks, split shot or anything for lunch. Doesn't matter though, really, does it? I'm just here to have some fun, catch some fish and relax. I'm sure I can borrow what I need from the other chaps here. They look a friendly bunch, especially those guys over there with the long poles sitting on the plastic boxes. They look really well organised, all in a long row like that. I'll just pop over and have a chat.'

The match angler[1]

'Unship one section, unship the next, and the next, it's only a skimmer,[2] let the elastic take the strain, lift the last section and swing the fish out of the water, don't need the net, don't have the time, got to keep the rhythm going... pole under arm, disgorger out from behind the ear, into the fish's mouth, wiggle, out with the hook, drop it into the net, check the hook with one hand and re-bait, single grain of corn and a caster cocktail, catching fish when all around me aren't, especially Jimmy with that bloke in the straw hat bending his ear – aaand ship the first section back out and then the next one, and the next, drop the float in and let it settle, pole balanced under arm, right hand into the bait box, handful of maggots out and into the catapult – PING – right on top of the float, dip, dip, strike, unship one section, unship the next and the next...'

1. *He's pole-fishing (see page 55).*
2. *A small silver fish, often a bream.*

The specimen hunter

'So where would I be, if I were a giant carp? All the racket from that match might have put him down, but there's an awful lot of bait in the water and some of it smells so good that his olfactories are all aquiver. He's going to be on the edge, just like me. Part of what's going on around him but also miraculously invisible, even to those who are right next to him. I'd put money that he's patrolling the reed margins on the other side of the lake to me, moving as I move, in tandem and in secret. Those reeds just knocked. There, they did it again. He's truffling his way along, looking for bloodworm and snails, the rich reek from the churned mud all around him. I'll take another step to the right, then another, never taking my eyes off the far bank. He does the same. Oblivious to everything else, we move in parallel along the ancient lines of the lake, each a mirror image of the other. We blend into the background silently like smoke, like...'

The old boy

'What the 'ell d'you think you're doing, creeping along the bank like that? Frightened the life out of me. Bad enough that lot have taken over half the lake for their daft match, then you come crashing along. I've been fishing here 40 years and this is all the respect I get. You look like one of them survivalists or something. You're not in the Territorials are you? My nephew went in the TA and he's still a horrible little squirt. Wait a minute, come back – you've trodden on my sandwiches...'

Species profile: The salmon

King of fish. Most anglers in the UK will never see a salmon that isn't on their plate – unless they go abroad. Salmon are born in fresh water and stay there for up to eight years before making their way down to the sea, which is where they bulk up for a further four years or so before returning to the same river – indeed the same tributary – they were born in, to spawn again.

Good for: The greatest, most expensive fight of your fishing life.

The dry-fly fisherman

'Dear Sirs, Despite the fact that your brochure and "web site" promise "giant rainbow trout" and "clarity of the water... fed by natural springs" and "an exclusive environment where the discerning fly angler can fill his creel" I find myself compelled to complain. Have you ever actually visited this water? It looks as though the lake is fed by the run-off from a brewery rather than the crystal waters of a spring. Perusing the shallows I find little insect life that my flies may imitate but many bright red round things that look like gobstoppers, and although I have cast diligently for several hours I have yet to raise a single fish. In closing I'd like to point out that some of the other anglers appear to be living here in a sort of tent city and that there's a burger van – *a burger van* – by the side of the lake, serving all-day breakfasts. Your sincerely, etc. P.S. The car park is also full of Fiestas.'

The miserable angler

'I suppose I'll have another cast, even though I don't really see the point. Even that bloke in the camouflage jacket hasn't caught anything and he's probably a much better angler than me. I don't know why I bother. I expect the bait's come off the hook. Feels like rain, too. These maggots look spoiled. I think I'm going to pack up now, no sense wasting the rest of the day – anyway I think I'm getting a cold.'

Homemade mosquito repellent

Mosquitoes can make an angler's life miserable. Try these two cheap alternatives to prevent bites.

First, mix together four tablespoons of baby oil and one tablespoon of disinfectant; then pour the mixture into a spray bottle. For a sweeter-smelling alternative, try mixing a tablespoon of vanilla extract with a small cup of water and then spraying that on.

The holiday angler

'This is the life. Son, pop this back to the man and see if he's got any ketchup, then wake your mum up and tell her to give you a beer from the fridge for me. If she says it's too early, tell her I said it doesn't matter, we're on holiday. Am I right? Good, off you go. Right, let's see what we can get out of here, the tackle shop bod said there were plenty of fish so when the boy gets back we'll have that burger and then have a go, am I right? Licence? Don't need one mate. This is one of those counties that doesn't bother with them – that's what the guy in the shop said, or someone did, I don't remember. Anyway, if you want my opinion, there shouldn't be any licences and the fishing should all be free. It's probably that lot in Brussels poking their noses in again where they're not wanted. People pay enough tax already. Am I right? There you are, son, about time. Good boy, now give me those and then pop back to the caravan and get the radio.'

One, two, three, four, five.
Once I caught a fish alive,
Six, seven, eight, nine, ten,
Then I let it go again.[1]
Why did you let it go?
Because it bit my finger so.
Which finger did it bite?
This little finger on the right.

Child's nursery rhyme, anonymous

1. Some anglers wonder if this is the first example of catch and release.

Species profile: The shad

Imagine a herring that thinks it's a salmon and thus lives part of its life in fresh water and the other part in the sea, and you've got the Thwaite and Allis shad. They mainly still spawn in the Solway, Usk, Wye and Severn rivers, and while not the most beautiful of fish, should be treated with the care and respect their rarity deserves.

Good for: Looking after carefully while we still can.

fish and country music

We've always thought that fishing and the 'music of pain' had lots in common – and so did these artists:

- 'The Five-Pound Bass' by Robert Earl Keen ('Jumped in my pickup, gave her the gas/Goin' out to catch a 5 lb bass.')
- 'Fishing Blues' by Taj Mahal ('Here's a little tip I would like to relate/A big fish bites if ya got good bait.')
- 'I'm Gonna Miss Her' by Brad Paisley ('Well I love her but I love to fish/I spend all day out on this lake and hell is all I catch.')

Gangs of small boys

'Wotcha mate, caught anything? Can I borrow your torch mate? What sort of fish are in here, mate? What bait you using? Got any bread, mate? What's that then, mate? Can my mate borrow your torch? Where's the best place to fish, mate? Have you got a light? My mate left his fags in the car, have you got any fags? Uh-oh, here comes the bloke – run!'

The bivvy boy

'How do you switch this on? OK, OK, got it. Hurrumph. Day two. No sign of Boris. Have baited the far bank liberally with strawberry boilies and tiger nuts stewed in beer and am fishing a single halibut pop-up on a braid hair rig on the first line, bolt rig on the second with a mega-dynamo pineapple dumbbell and a squid n' tutti frutti pairing on the third.[1] Been rubbish so far, no proper runs, just loads of tench snaffling the bait, up to about 9 lb. Waste of time. Lad next door reckons Boris is usually anyone's this time of year, just as it's starting to get cold. Wants to bulk up for the winter and always fancies a bit of a scoff, especially as it gets dark. Knowing my luck it'll be just as I'm settling down to a nice chicken tikka masala with all the trimmings. This new stove is the business. Right, how does this work? Store. Upload. Tab, tab, select YouTube. Tag "carp" "fishing" "specimen". Uploading. Right, give it half an hour and see how many hits I've got.'

1. Feel free to replace these unlikely-sounding baits with some of your own.

157

The predator

'People ask me why I fish with my dog. Two reasons. First, he's better company than most of the people I know. Second, he's got a bit of a temper and he keeps other anglers away so I can get some peace. I don't come fishing to talk to other people. You need to be able to focus in this game, especially with the lake like Piccadilly Circus. Haven't seen any sign so far and if there's a pike about those ruddy match anglers will let me know – they won't stop bellyaching about it. What I need is a few little roach for livebait. I can sling a bung out on the edge of the island here and pick up any passing pike as they move up the lake through the narrow channel and onto the smaller fish being attracted by all that bait.'

The fishing loffin

'Wind from the south-west, strong enough to blow food across to this corner, so that's a good start. It'll probably nudge the thermocline layer towards the bottom a tad and the fish will follow that. Pop the thermometer in the water – 7 degrees centigrade. Perfect. Sky looks like rain in a bit which means the pressure will drop and oxygen levels in the water will rise; we need the air pressure to be below 1000 millibars.'

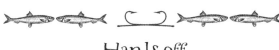

Hands off

The following fish are protected in Great Britain and must not be fished for intentionally.

Allis shad – *Alosa alosa*

Burbot – *Lota lota*

Schelly, powan or gwyniad – *Coregonus lavaretus*

Sturgeon – *Acipenser sturio*

Vendace – *Coregonus albula*

The salmon angler

'That's 45 day tickets at £7.50 a shot and another 12 at £12 for two rods; one fly-fishing afternoon ticket with a three-fish limit for £16; 15 all-day breakfasts at £6 a go, 200 cups of tea at 80 pence each, 150 coffees at £1.10, 25 bacon butties at £3.50 a go. Six caravans at £50 a night, plus £10 for the electric hookup and another £3 a day for residents' preferred parking. Comes to £1,378. That'll get me a couple of full days on the Tweed with a guide, use of fly/spinning rods and reels, lines, leaders, and all the flies and lures I need. They'll chuck in waders and a wading staff and I'll still have plenty left over for accommodation, tips and a few glasses of the Macallan. "Yes, sir, can I see your ticket? Just the two of you for the afternoon? That'll be £6 for yourself and £4 for the lad." No, thank *you* very much.'

The club angler

'Work party did a good job clearing up these banks last weekend, pity it's always the same faces, club could do with some new blood to help out the committee a bit. Must get the keys back from John and make sure the gate's shut after everyone leaves. Might need to check a few membership cards later on – don't like the look of those lads and I bet they're not members. Wish people would pick up behind themselves and not treat the place like a rubbish tip. Oi, shouldn't that dog be on a leash?'

The lucky angler

'Right, I'm going to reel in, just let the float sit there for a second while I pour a cup of tea and have a ginger nut. No sense bringing it in completely and having to re-bait, it'll be fine for a second or two. Blast, my dunking's got a bit rusty, that's half the biscuit I've dropped in there. Let me fish it out with my fingers. Ouch, that's hot. And that. Ouch. Have to remember there'll be bits at the bottom. Right, let's lift the tackle out of the water and... what's this? Stone me, feels like another really good roach.'

The angling author

'The lake is even more beautiful than usual this evening, and once again I have it to myself. I'll probably start here under the willows, my back to the bark of this sturdy tree, throw in a few loose offerings and then wait for the fish to move over my bait. I'm using simple float tackle today and as the silence gathers around me I recall other nights at this secluded pool where my only light was lunar, my only companion the barn owl who hunts, like me, in the shadows...'

Species profile: The tench

Forever associated with June 16th,[1] the tench has olive skin as smooth as soap, a large paddle-like tail and a lovely little red eye. Hard fighting, it prefers still water but will thrive in sluggish rivers and is particularly partial to sweetcorn or red worms.

Good for: It's the first 'proper' fish that many anglers ever catch.

1. The pursuit of tench is traditionally linked to June the 16th, the old opening day of the coarse-fishing season after a three-month break.

The angling widow

'The downside? Maggots in the fridge. Mud tracked over my hall carpet every weekend. Nets left out in the sun. Saucepans ruined by his secret bait 'experiments'. (Once I had to throw the food processor away). The dog going bonkers after getting into the bin and eating all that hemp. My mother sat on a treble hook once. The fact that he never washes his hands. That time he still had slime in his hair when he came to bed. The upside? I suppose it gets him out of the house.'

So that's our selection of ordinary, everyday anglers (with overdue apologies to all concerned), but what about the extraordinary ones? In the final chapter we doff our caps to those fishermen who made a difference, the angling legends.

' The wonder of the world
The beauty and the power,
The shapes of things,
Their colours, lights and shades,
These I saw.
Look ye also while life lasts. '

Anonymous

This quotation was used by 'BB' in all
his books. It's said to be found on a
memorial to Alexander Morton, a
Scottish Victorian industrialist.

CHAPTER EIGHT

FISHING LEGENDS

ny list of this type is bound to attract as many brickbats as it does bouquets, but that doesn't mean we shouldn't attempt it. Angling is full of characters, many of whom have advanced the sport through their innovations, others by their organisational skills and determination – some because they are able to reflect angling's joyful mystery in their writing and drawing. This list is a personal one – and we're sure you'll have your own – but in vaguely chronological order, ladies and gentlemen, please raise your rods to:

Izaak Walton (1593–1683)

The father of angling and still one of the fishermen that most other fishermen would fancy having a pint with, if only because even at a first meeting there would be no awkward silences in the conversation – and maybe even some lusty singing before the evening was out. Lord, that man loved to talk, framing his masterpiece, *The Compleat Angler*, first published in 1653, as a discourse between sportsmen and peppering it with a shambolic mix of country wisdom, old wives' tales, practical advice and sound sense. If he were alive today, Walton would probably have his own TV show on a cable channel. Or at least a radio phone-in.

Few people come to Walton by themselves, rather he's recommended in the pages of other angling books, and here is his greatest legacy. *The Compleat Angler* informs and infuses the content of so many other books that – say what you like about its content and accuracy (and many do) – it's probably the most influential angling book ever written. Hence his appearance in these pages.

H. T. Sheringham (1876–1930)

Unlike many of his contemporaries who felt obliged to elevate one kind of fishing over another, Sheringham was an all-rounder. In the introduction to his book, *Coarse Fishing*, published in 1912, he wrote: 'Salmon fishing is good, trout fishing is good; but to the complete angler neither is intrinsically better than the pursuit of roach or tench or perch or pike.'

These were the sentiments he expressed in some of the finest and longest-lasting angling books of the age – *An Angler's Hour* (1905), *An Open Creel* (1910), *Trout Fishing: Memories and Morals* (1920) and *Fishing: Its Cause, Treatment and Cure* (1923) – writing with such a light touch and self-deprecating humour that the result is a body of work to stand with angling's finest. Many people came to Sheringham as a result of his 27-year stint as the angling editor of *The Field* magazine, where once again he transformed what can so often deteriorate into a set of do-this, do-that instructionals into genuine, involving literature. Sheringham wrote about angling as if it mattered, and in this – like so many other things – he was right.

Denys Watkins-Pitchford or 'BB' (1905-1990)

Best known by his nom de plume, 'BB', Watkins-Pitchford wrote a series of successful children's books, the most famous of which – *The Little Grey Men* – won the Carnegie Medal for the most outstanding children's book in 1942. He illustrated his own work (he taught art at Rugby public school) and is responsible for *The Fisherman's Bedside Book*, first published in 1945, which brought together some of the finest angling writing of the time and remains one of fishing's best anthologies; at 568 pages, 174 stories and 80 authors, it's good value too.

He took his name from the gauge of pellet gun used to shoot geese (and later loved by small boys of all persuasions before such things were frowned upon) and thought of himself more as a writer of country matters. He still wrote the book that inspired a generation of carp anglers, however – *Confessions of a Carp Fisher* (1951) – which was written at a time when carp were considered almost uncatchable and when the British record stood at a 'mere' 26 lb (11.8 kg).

We have our reservations about the way carp angling has come to dominate the sport in the UK, but we have none about this wonderful and inspirational author.

G. E. M. Skues (1858-1949)

Enough authors already! Let's meet a real angler and a real innovator. George Edward MacKenzie Skues is credited with transforming fly fishing, courtesy of his 'invention' – the nymph. At a time when dry-fly fishing ruled the roost and wet flies were impressionistic approximations of God-knew-what, Skues started to think of flies in terms of tails, ribs, abdomens, wing cases and thoraxes; in other words, what the actual individual insects looked like.

For his trouble, his contemporaries – dry-fly anglers all – who fished the same stretch of the river Itchen, Hampshire, made life so uncomfortable for him that he upped sticks and began fishing elsewhere; it must have been miserable and Skues never lost his love for the river – one of his best books *Side-Lines, Side-Lights & Reflections*, is dedicated simply

'To ITCHEN'. In his will, he requested that his ashes be scattered there.

Writing in *Salmon & Trout Magazine* in July 1924, he observed: 'it is, I think, clear that there is no finality in fly dressing for trout but a field for endless experiment and advance.' Skues certainly did his bit.

Bernard Venables (1907–2001)

Bernard Venables shares this page with his greatest creation, Mr Crabtree, a cartoon character created for the *Daily Mirror* newspaper who, with his son Peter, taught two generations of anglers how to fish through a series of weekly strips. Shadowing the angling year, the pair start in winter, fishing a deep eddy, progress through summer sessions for tench, carp and bream, into autumn with rudd, barbel, roach, dace, perch, chub and pike, before finishing with three lovely trout. Crabtree had begun life as a gardening strip but that was too seasonal a subject for regular work and Venables suggested taking him fishing instead. Angling's first star was born.

Modern anglers may wince occasionally – for example when Crabtree pronounces on a perch, 'There, isn't he lovely? About a pound. And what a delicious meal he'll make.' – but the stories and strips resonate to this day, so much so that it's easy to forget Venables' contribution elsewhere: wonderful colour paintings of fish, the founding of *Angling Times*, the sport's pre-eminent newspaper and *Creel*, a before-its-time magazine which featured the work of Dick Walker, Fred Taylor, Fred Buller, Clive Gammon, 'BB' and others.

Hugh Faulkus (1917–1996)

Faulkus wasn't just a master angler, he was an extraordinary amalgam of instructor, observer and author. Maybe it was his 'real job' as a film maker with the BBC's Natural History Unit that taught him the value of seeing things in the round and the gift to explain them to anybody. He'd already learned patience in his four years as a POW during World War II (though Faulkus did not take to imprisonment and it's said he caught and cooked the camp commander's cat).

He's best remembered as a sea-trout angler and put much (though probably not all) his knowledge down in *Sea Trout; A Guide to Success* (1962), a bible for lovers of this singular fish, who often see themselves as something of a breed apart from other anglers – many moving close to their favourite rivers so they can fish whenever the sea trout run, at the drop of a hat.

And if that wasn't enough, with Fred Buller, Faulkus co-authored the remarkable book – or should that be encyclopaedia? – *Freshwater Fishing*, first published in 1975, and still one of the best practical guides to fish and fishing techniques; good recipes, too.

Dick Walker (1918–1985)

In an age where many anglers thought that luck and a kind of dogged persistence would get them through somehow, Richard Walker brought an engineer's rigour to angling and a keenness to discover why fish behaved as they did – and how that understanding could be turned to the angler's advantage.

Species profile: The trout

For many anglers, the trout is more than just a fish – or collection of different fishes. It is a religion, part of a mystical experience that's bound up in the rhythmic repetition of fly casting, the beauty – generally – of the surroundings, the turning of the seasons, the languid disdain of the fish (in a moment so unpredictably transformed into ferocity), the science and art of fly tying, of choosing the right fly, and more.[1]

To fish for trout is to understand how yearning and despair, triumph and tantrums can coexist within the same person in a matter of moments; we've seen fly fishermen turn from being utterly at peace with the world to virtually jumping up and down on their own rods. It's like watching someone turn into a werewolf.

As to the fish themselves, most anglers in the UK catch rainbow trout or brown trout; some rivers have a run of sea trout and many Scottish lochs are home to large, angry ferox trout – both of these are brown trout who've taken a wrong turn and wandered down to the sea or found themselves in an environment where the main food source is other, smaller fish.

Good for: Breaking anglers' hearts.

1. *Most coarse anglers think trout stupid and a nuisance – unless they're big enough to eat.*

 173

He takes his place here for many reasons. He held the British carp record for 30 years (see page 123), he invented the electronic bite alarm and the Arlesey bomb (a clever tear-shaped weight with a swivel that flew through the air, didn't snag and reduced line twist); he designed rods, specifically the Mark IV which was built to handle big carp, and invented all manner of end tackle and rigs. Much of this was set down in *Still Water Angling* (1953), still considered by many to be the only fishing book you need ever read (present company excepted); and he wrote a column in *Angling Times* for thirty years which was always informative and often controversial.

Walker changed the way anglers caught big fish forever – transforming it from a sequence of chance and lucky guesses into a deliberate act – and is arguably the single most influential angler of all time.

Recipe: fried trout

'Take two or three eggs, more or less according as you have fish to fry, take the fish and cut it in thin slices, lie it upon a board, rub the eggs over it with a feather, and strow on a little flour and salt, fry it in fine drippings or butter, let the drippings be very hot before you put in the fish, but do not let it burn, if you do it will make the fish black; when the fish is in the pan, you may do the other side with the egg, and as you fry it lay it to drain before the fire till all be fried, then it is ready for use.'

English Housewifery, published in 1764

The missed bite

'The bite that occurs when one attempts to light up a cigarette or pipe, or attempts to attend to the inner man. Missed – barring occasional flukes.'

'Faddist' (Edward Ensom) writing about different types of bite and their likely outcome, in *Roach Fishing, A Complete Manual of the Art of Angling for Roach*

Reverend Edward C. Alston
(c.1890-1977)

The angling legend that no one's ever heard of, Alston survived the Great War as a junior officer and afterwards left the army to be ordained as a priest in the Church of England in 1924. He became the vicar of Thetford, an old market town in Norfolk, and there rediscovered his boyhood love of fishing.

He wrote no books or magazine articles and didn't invent any tackle or techniques that we know of, yet his name crops up regularly in the record books, most notably for a 4 lb 8 oz (2 kg) rudd (he caught another the same day in 1933 of 'only' 4 lb 4 oz) and a 7 lb 8 oz (3.4 kg) tench, both British records. Alston's technique was simple. Having noticed that his local pond was empty of fish but rich in the food they like, he took himself to another lake, purchased some rudd and tench of a good size and then put them in the first lake. Then he waited.

When Alston started to hear stories of large fish being caught from the lake by small boys he returned, and thus were his mighty catches

made. But he didn't land everything and would remember with regret the tench he lost – he estimated it would have weighed 10 lb (4.5 kg).

Ivan Marks (1936–2004)

We could have invited any number of match anglers to the top table – particularly Kevin Ashurst – but in the end, Ivan Marks gets the nod because of the way he was dubbed 'angling's first superstar' by the *Angling Times*. Angling isn't necessarily known for its rebels, but the young Marks and his mates from Leicester Angling Society brought exuberance and fresh ideas to the rather strait-laced match angling scene of the late 60s.

Marks was a voracious angler who would fish anywhere, any time, and usually do better than those around him. He fished for the national team, won the Great Ouse championship three times and gained many other individual winner's medals – including a silver at the 1976 World Championships, a trophy he both loved and hated; he would also sometimes fish all-comer matches where 1,000 anglers would pitch up and do their worst – and win.

Wrongly characterised by some as 'just' a bream man, Marks was master of the waggler, the stick, the bomb and the feeder and could winkle fish out of the most difficult waters; he once told *Angling Times* he was 'just an ordinary bloke who could fish a bit.'

John Wilson (b.1954)

One-time ship's hairdresser, merchant navyman and printer who became the face of modern angling courtesy of a long-running series of TV shows (the best known, *Go Fishing*, ran from 1986 to 2002) and the catchphrases that peppered them. Infectious and enthusiastic, Wilson's cries of 'Hello, we're in!' or 'That's a nice fish,' or ;no, no, no!' and of course 'That is a clonker!' have been adopted by a generation of anglers (though no one else seems to have perfected that cackling head-back laugh).

Despite the lo-fi, low-budget feel of many of Wilson's programmes, he's an accomplished presenter, knows how to narrate so the viewer understands what's going on (too many TV anglers forget to talk to the camera at key

moments) and heaven knows, he can catch fish; just as important, he seems as happy catching roach and perch as he does sturgeon and Nile perch.

Many anglers also have reason to thank Wilson for his range of inexpensive signature rods and the original Avon/quiver – which we still own by the way – is said to be the best selling fishing rod of all time.

Bob Nudd (b.1944)

One of the angling world's most recognisable characters, thanks to his ever-present white flat cap and red tops, Bob Nudd is also its most successful sportsman, four times individual world champion in 1990, 1991, 1994 and 1999, and despite the cheerful grin and easy manner, one of the most competitive anglers ever. It's said he would have won BBC TV's Sports Personality of the Year award in 1991 but for a technicality – or perhaps because angling isn't accepted as a sport by many – and also received an MBE for services to angling. Considered by many to be the master of pole fishing.

Chris Yates (b.1948)

Four words – *A Passion For Angling*. Chris Yates features here thanks to his turn as one of a pair of eccentric anglers in the six-part BBC TV series, famous for its stunning camera work (courtesy of Hugh '*Kingdom Of The Ice Bear*' Miles), an emotional narration by actor and angler Bernard Cribbins, and Jennie Muskett's lovely orchestral soundtrack. Although fellow angler Bob James caught most of the big fish, it was Yates who won the angling nation's heart, thanks in the main to his unusual approach – antique tackle, odd clothing, a love of wicker and quaint, wood-burning kettles – and his sense that angling belongs to a wider tradition of pure enjoyment, whether fish are caught or not.

Yates has also produced some of the most personal and evocative modern angling books – notably *Casting at the Sun*, published in 1986 – and was one of the founders of *Waterlog*, a conscious attempt to create a more literary, reflective style of angling magazine that kicked against the modern trend for presenting angling as if it was something to be consumed, like fast food.

And lest we forget, Yates also held the British carp record for may years with a massive 51 lb (23 kg) fish, caught – as was Walker's record before it – from the tiny pool at Redmire.

The Unknown Angler

It's an old trick – but nevertheless a good one – for authors to insert themselves into the narrative at some point, and where else can you do it if not on the last page of the book? So here's to us, the anglers no one will ever hear of – the anglers who run clubs and syndicates, who teach kids to fish, pick up litter when they see it, look after the fish they catch and cherish their habitat, who love the solitary hours by the water in all weathers as much as they love a joke and a story over a beer; here's to the anglers who come back to fishing and those who never leave, to those who catch and those who don't, to Chick and Ray and Sean and you and we, and all the unknown anglers everywhere. Here's to us.

Glossary

Arlesey bomb Tear-shaped weight with a built-in swivel perfected by Richard Walker for use on Arlesey lake.

baiting needle Device used to attach soft baits (usually boilies) to a short length of line that hangs clear of the hook.

barbless Hook without bars; just as good and easier to remove from a fish's mouth.

base mix The base to which you add flavours and oils to make boilies. Semolina and soya flour is a good base mix, for example.

bivvy Small tent used by anglers fishing through the night or in bad weather.

boilie Round, man-made bait primarily designed to catch carp; also works for tench, barbel and bream.

braid Tough line that doesn't abrade or stretch, is thinner than traditional fishing line but more visible.

breaking strain The amount of force you need to apply to fishing line before it snaps.

bubble float Little plastic ball with removable stoppers so you can add water and make it heavier; used as a float when surface-fishing for carp or live-baiting for pike.

bung Float the size and shape of an egg, used for pike fishing.

cane Actually split cane, a technique for making fishing rods out of six slim triangular lengths of bamboo cane, glued together lengthways to form a hexagon.

caster The pupal stage of a maggot, when it forms a hard shell before turning into a fly.

cocktail Two baits on the same hook, for example a grain of sweetcorn and a maggot.

dapping Poking a rod out over the edge of a lake or river and lowering the bait onto the surface of the water.

disgorger Tool for removing the hook from a fish's mouth; some look like medical forceps, others like slim tubes with a notch at the business end which – when slid down the line – can extract a hook from a fish's throat.

drag The spools on most modern reels are fixed and do not turn; drag settings allow you to adjust the tension on the spool so that, should a fish pull particularly hard, the spool will turn and release line grudgingly. The trick is to set the drag so it kicks in just before the breaking strain of the line is reached.

feeder A cotton-reel-sized cage with a weight, attached to the line near the hook; fill it with groundbait, and this will be slowly released around the hook to attract fish.

groundbait Mix of various ingredients, made into balls and thrown into the water to attract fish without actually filling them up.

hair rig clever way of attaching a bait to a hook via a short stretch of line; means you don't actually put the hook in the bait and is said to result in more fish hooked.

hooklength Last stretch of line to the hook; may be lighter and thinner than the mainline.

hook tyer Device for attaching a hook to a length of line; useful for complex knots or when using smaller hooks.

lateral line Horizontal row of scales that helps a fish sense what's going on around it.

leader Length of tapered line that sits between the thick, heavy fly line and the finer tippet onto which you tie the fly.

ledger A weight used to cast a bait and then carry it down to the bottom of a lake or river.

livebait Literally hooking a live small fish to attract a predator like a pike or zander.

plummet Tear-shaped weight used to help anglers find the depth of the water they're going to fish.

pop-up A buoyant bait that rises off the bottom; useful for fishing silty, muddy-bottomed lakes and rivers.

quiver tip A rod tip that's usually white with a brightly-coloured top and is lighter or more sensitive than the rest of the rod; used for ledgering. Tighten up to the bait so the tip bends slightly and then watch for pulls and tugs.

ratchet Mechanism for slowing down a free-spinning centrepin reel so that a fish can't take line so easily.

riparian Applies to the person who owns the land adjoining a watercourse.

rod rest Metal pole into which you screw a v-shaped top on which you can rest your rod; sometimes called a bank stick.

skimmer A small silver fish, usually a bream.

snap tackle Length of wire with two treble hooks attached about a finger-length apart; used for hooking live fish.

split shot Small, round soft weights, split two thirds of the way through, which can be pinched onto the line to balance, for example, a float.

stick float What you might call an old-fashioned float, bulbous in the middle and thinner at the top and bottom.

test curve The amount of weight that, when applied to a rod, will bend it into a 90-degree curve.

thermocline Thin, distinct layer of water which changes temperature more rapidly with depth than the water above or below it.

tippet Short length of line of constant diameter used in fly fishing; one end is tied to a leader, the other to the fly.

trail Distance between the last weight in a rig (usually ledger but can be float) and the hook.

trot To let a float drift downstream with the current of the river, releasing line from the reel as it goes.

waggler A straight float (which may have a small inset tip) attached by the bottom only to the line and used for stillwater fishing.

wet sack protective, porous, sealed bag which can be staked to the bank and used to keep large fish safe in the water for a short time.

wobbling A way of hooking a deadbait so that when it's retrieved it wobbles through the water like an injured fish.

185

A very peculiar angling timeline

Prehistory Job is admonished that he may as well 'try and catch Leviathan with a hook as thwart God's will.'

2,000 BC Egyptians are fishing with rod, line and hook.

800 BC Odysseus and his men catch and eat fish as a last resort before starving.

900 AD Chinese poet Li Yu describes fishing under a battalion of plum trees.

1st Century AD The ichthys fish symbol is used by early Christians to identify each other.

2nd Century AD Macedonians described going fly fishing.

4th Century AD European Celts attribute powers of prophecy to the salmon; inhabitants of Rapa Nui (Easter Island) carve fish hooks from bone.

10th Century AD Aelfric, an English monk, writes his *Colloquy* to teach students Latin; fishermen appear as characters in his dialogues.

13th Century AD Carp are first introduced to England by monks, who keep them in small stewponds for food; turkeys arrive at same time (perhaps they became our favourite Xmas treat because they aren't so hard to catch).

1486 *A treatyse of fysshynge wyth an Angle* by Dam Julyans Barnes appears; it's fishing's first how-to book.

1651 *Barker's Delight or The Art of Angling* published.

1653 Izaak Walton's *The Compleat Angler* published.

1860 Joseph Malin opens England's first fish and chip shop; brown trout introduced into New Zealand.

1880s Rainbow trout introduced to the UK from America ('Yo, how you doin'?!').

1901–1910 Gudgeon parties attended by fashionable ladies and gentlemen become popular on the river Thames.

1903 National Federation of Anglers is founded.

1914 Theodore Roosevelt sees starving piranhas scoff a small cow in a staged feeding frenzy for tourists; mud sticks.

1951 Dick Walker designs the most famous rod in angling history – the Mark IV.

1952 Pete Thomas nearly catches Clarissa, but fishing four feet (1.2 m) away Dick Walker does instead; she's a British record 44 lb (20 kg) carp.

1953 *Still Water Angling* by Dick Walker is published, arguably the single most influential angling book of modern times.

1970s Catfish first introduced to the Ebro river system in Spain.

1971 The author flukes his first barbel on the river Thames at Windsor while fishing 'for anything'.

1980 Chris Yates catches 'the Bishop', at 51½ lbs (23.4 kg) a new British record carp, again from Redmire Pool.

1990 Bob Nudd becomes individual world champion angler; he wins it again another three times.

1994 Close season on still waters abolished – in typical, short-sighted fashion.

2007 The seven-billionth can of Spam – the original luncheon meat – is sold.

2009 The Angling Trust established as a national body speaking for all anglers in the UK; you should join – www.anglingtrust.net

July 2009 Benson, the monster carp, is found dead. The story is front-page news.

2011 Barbel begin to breed naturally in the river Don, in England's north-east; they may soon become self-sustaining. Fingers crossed.

Index

Cricket
A Very Peculiar History
With added googlies
Jim Pipe
ISBN: 978-1-908177-90-2

The Olympics
A Very Peculiar History
With added medals
David Arscott
ISBN: 978-1-907184-78-9

The 60's
A Very Peculiar History
With added flower power
David Arscott
ISBN: 978-1-908177-92-6

London
A Very Peculiar History
With added jellied eels
Jim Pipe
ISBN: 978-1-907184-26-0

Great Britons
A Very Peculiar History
with added stiff upper lip
Ian Graham
ISBN: 978-1-907184-59-8

Vampires
A Very Peculiar History
With added Bite
Fiona Macdonald
ISBN: 978-1-907184-39-0

World War II
A Very Peculiar History
Jim Pipe
ISBN: 978-1-908177-97-1

Golf
A Very Peculiar History
With NO added bogeys
David Arscott
ISBN: 978-1-907184-75-8

The World Cup
A Very Peculiar History
With NO added Time
David Arscott
ISBN: 978-1-907184-38-3

Whisky
A Very Peculiar History
A wee drop o' the hard stuff
Fiona Macdonald
ISBN: 978-1-907184-76-5

Titanic
A Very Peculiar History
With added iceberg
Jim Pipe
ISBN: 978-1-907184-87-1

Christmas
A Very Peculiar History
With Lashings of Second
Helpings
Fiona Macdonald
ISBN: 978-1-907184-50-5

Queen Elizabeth II
A Very Peculiar History
60 Years a Queen
David Arscott
ISBN: 978-1-908177-50-6

Robert Burns
A Very Peculiar History
With the bard's own rhymes
Fiona Macdonald
ISBN: 978-1-908177-71-1